MAKING PEACE

Photographs & Interviews
with Peacemakers in the United States

Arthur Dahl

with a foreword by Daniel Berrigan

SHEED & WARD

Cover design by Franz Altschuler

Printed in the United States of America, 1990

Library of Congress Cataloging-in-Publication Data

Dahl, Arthur H.
  Making peace.

  1. Pacifists—Interviews. 2. Pacifists—Portraits.
I. Title.
JX 1961. U6D34 1990 327.1'72 88-42606

ISBN: 1-55612-321-3

Published by: Sheed & Ward
                 115 E. Armour Blvd. P.O. Box 419492
                 Kansas City, MO 64141- 6492

To order, call: (800) 333-7373

Printed on acid free paper

Dedicated
to the continuation of
life on this planet
and all forces
working together in the
struggle for it.

"All it takes for
evil to flourish is
for a few good
(persons) to do nothing."

Edmund Burke

"There is no way in which a country can satisfy the craving for absolute security – but it can bankrupt itself, morally and economically, in attempting to reach that illusory goal through arms alone . . . Every gun that is made, every warship launched, every rocket fired, signifies in the final sense a theft from those who are hungry and are not fed, those who are cold and are not clothed. This world in arms is not spending money alone. It is spending the sweat of its laborers, the genius of its scientists, the hopes of its children."

Dwight David Eisenhower

Acknowledgements

In any project of this duration one encounters not only the proverbial mountains and valleys, but also, at crucial junctures, certain persons who appear in the life of it – sustaining and energizing – and without whom things might not have continued. Besides those key individuals mentioned in the Introduction others include: my friend and pastor, David Chevrier, and unfailing source of encouragement and surprise; Madeline Callahan, John Deedy, Kathy Elliott, Ingeborg Lauterstein and David Wise, who were all clear in their vision, and clearly the right persons, at the right places, at the right times; Suzanne Kurman, transcriber and authors' helper, championed the work beyond expectation, as did Denise Salah.

Innumerable individuals pointed me in the direction of others; special among these were: Carol Bobrow, Gina Covina, Nancy Rockwell and Ginny Yancy.

During almost a year's travel I was afforded friendship and hospitality by countless communities and individuals. Some among them were: Catholic Worker houses in ten cities; the Erie Benedictine community; Dick Johnson, Gail Robinson, Janice and David Rogers, Prof. Herbert Rothschild, John and Jean Sizemore, Dr. and Mrs. Tom Wesson.

The Mundelein College Learning Resource Center, Chicago, and The Sawyer Free Library, Gloucester, Massachusetts, both gave me space in which to work, for which I am grateful.

Helen Stephenson, of the Authors Guild, and Paul Vanderbilt, of the Wisconsin State Historical Society, both offered technical expertise and enthusiasm, as did my longtime friend, who helped in the design of this book, Franz Altschuler.

To all these named, and all others, I offer my deepest appreciation, gratitude, and thanks.

In addition to the *Making Peace* book, *Making Peace* exists as a traveling exhibition. The traveling exhibition has received generous support and sponsorship from: the Boston Globe Foundation; Greater Boston Physicians for Social Responsibility (GBPSR); the Illinois Arts Council, a state agency; International Physicians for the Prevention of Nuclear War (IPPNW); Massachusetts Department of Environmental Management –

Massachusetts Heritage State Parks; Neilsen-Bainbridge Corporation.
   For information about how to arrange the *Making Peace* exhibit for your community, please contact the exhibit's original sponsor:

GBPSR (Greater Boston Physicians for Social Responsibility)
19 Garden St.
Cambridge, Massachusetts 02138
617/497-7440

Or you may contact the author directly:

Arthur H. Dahl
1814 N. Paulina St.
Chicago, Illinois 60622
312/772-6892

Contents

Foreword

What an admirable American document Arthur Dahl has compiled; a sense of place, ordinary people talking up a storm, their comments and observations often eloquent, humorous, pointed, quick to the mark. "In our town," one of those interviewed declares, "the dogs and cats know the dogs and cats."

The speakers mostly go with old John Dewey, who understood that the American character leaned toward the proof of the pudding, not the pitch of the cook. Like pragmatist Dewey, they're strong for education, but only of a certain kind, of which they know more than something; education that puts hands and hearts in motion in the intractable world. You can't know something without doing something about what you've learned; this, they imply, is the saving grace in a graceless time.

Time and again, delightful aphorisms and down-home wisdom leap from the page. These Americans, generally unheard from, despised even (like most of us), their political voice silenced by a rapacious, bellicose, deceitful gang at the top, are not cowed; not in the least. They take things in hand; they find ways of getting peace moving. They talk to neighbors, meet in homes, write tracts, vigil and fast and raise an outcry as best they can. Sometimes they get arrested. Like many of us.

Dahl, the photographer and interviewer, has the good sense to let the people speak for themselves. I thought, as I pondered his splendid evocation of these lives, "Here's an artist who knows something about art."

Knows what? In the first place, the task is to learn from people, to let people talk; whether in Minneapolis or Boston, in cities or villages or farms. Prime the talk, encourage people who quite possibly have never encountered anyone who would listen to them, people whose peacemaking, even when it was ignored, remained solid and patient and cheerful.

Dahl went, as he tells, not to the big names. He heard of someone; it seemed as though every person he met led him to eight or nine others. Something astonishing, heartening: folk concerned about peace, working for peace, were scattered everywhere across the land, sowing seeds, keeping at it.

To be sure, no one of them claims to be turning around the monstrous tide of waste and anomie and betrayal and death-as-usual. Who could claim that?

They understood, those rural and small town and big town folk, that the point was to keep at it, not to give up, to get the message across to a few, to let the good seed take root in its own time.

The reasoning proves sound. If you believe strongly enough in something, and what you believe makes sense, others will cock an ear. A good thing goes further, a law of nature. Goodness diffuses itself, the philosopher said long ago. On the other hand, a good thing, good news, purpose, insight, if long bottled up, turns sour.

So the book took shape. In many pockets and corners of the country, many found time for Dahl, and he for them; a tribute to both sides. His insight, he shortly found, was valid; the American hunger for peace, for an end to political and moral idiocy, ran deep, to the bone; ran far, a very Mississippi of the spirit. He followed where it led.

A common note, and startling. The deep changes that occurred in people started with a kind of hunch, a guess. They describe it that way, time and again. Something was wrong in the conduct of the country's affairs. People were being hoodwinked; decisions were made at the top, in secret, and stayed there. Money was allocated, money was denied. The rich got richer, the arms-makers grew bloated and arrogant, a power unto themselves. You learned about such decisions long after the fact, when at all. Then you were stuck with things you had no part in creating – weaponry and waste. The anger is palpable and correct.

Who are these officials who take charge behind closed doors? Charge of our planet, charge of our children's lives? And so bring us, heedless and headlong, to the edge of disaster? By what right? And who are we after all? Children? We who raise families, work the land, respect one another, pinch pennies to get the young through school?

It was outrageous, everything adrift. Those responsible were destroying political maturity, were mocking grown men and women, treating them like children in a nursery.

Worse – it was as though some surreptitious, sauve Big Daddy had seized the keys of creation, piled up weapons at every hand, squandered our money, contemned the poor – and remained through it all grandly superior, above the wreckage, totally unaccountable.

A number of the stories read like religious conversion tales. Insight leads to crisis. America simply was not working; not even for those for who, as flannel mouths reminded, America was designed to work well. America, with you (us) in mind. So they said.

The conversion stories, sometimes hilarious, sometimes harrowing, seem to me totally American. Moreover, they are faithful to an older, biblical tradition – which is to say, peacemaking, like its fierce opposite, warmaking (and yet its brother, as Cain to Abel). Warmaking and peacemaking, in contention, start deep within the soul.

At the end, or at some time when the end is taking form, the choices narrow. One can hate or love, murder or embrace, No other principals appear in the arena except these two; to claim the day, the soul's turf. A skirmish of the spirits: On the one hand, the old ways, the way of the culture, the way we kill and die; since the beginning, that validation and blessing, time the great irrefutable proof, the past on our side. The dead on our side, who have died in war and rise again from the dead, their fervor and thirst for glory in no way quenched. On our part the appetites, the fevers and chills, the inevitability of things as they are ("there'll always be war, there always has been war"), the flags, the graves, the odes, the anthems, the Fourths of July.

One person tells his story in the name of all. He had it made; so did his family. Presumably things would go on that way, time was a cornucopian *in saecula saeculorum*. He lived in a comfortable affluent suburb. The home was adjacent to a presumably comfortable affluent cemetery. And one day, a minister friend asked him in passing; "Do you want to be buried there?"

By his own word, that did it. The question was not where his bones would be finally deposited. The question struck home as a statement, flat: "I am already dead and buried. This, and not the cars, the boat, the decor, the assured income, this is the truest truth about my life."

And then of course, Dewey; for the minister's question is an American one. What shall I do to relieve this horror to which I have been condemned, or have condemned myself?

It is a long time since we have not been ashamed to be Americans. This is the deadly legacy of the decade. Our honor has been stolen from us, our history, our sense of decency, our love for one another, our understanding that the world and its events rightly understood, are in our hands. Not theirs.

We have given our world over to thieves and scoundrels and deceivers. Someone says to Dahl, "I once thought of the arms race as middle class welfare; now I know it is organized crime." Exactly.

Dahl stresses in his introduction that he deliberately limited the scope of his interviews. No clergy, no heavies.

He left me wondering—why no academics? Perhaps Dewey, and numbers of decent Americans, have survived, indeed surpassed, the professors. If this is true, and experience leads me to believe it is, then the peace movement and, by implication, the entire realm of serious dissent, are in different hands than commonly supposed.

DANIEL BERRIGAN

Arthur Dahl

Classically trained in photography, having studied with Joseph Jachna, Aaron Siskind, and Ansel Adams, Arthur Dahl long has been involved in the politics of everyday life. He was born and raised in Chicago, where he now lives.

Hold fast to dreams
For if dreams die
Life is a broken-winged bird
That cannot fly.

Langston Hughes

On June 11, 1982, I found myself on a bus with the American Friends Service Committee traveling from Chicago to New York for the great Peace Rally the following day. For me this trip represented a return to social action after almost a decade of withdrawal, of quietness, during "the silent seventies," the Nixon years. Looking back, I realize this trip was a new beginning.

I remember arriving in New York that Saturday morning of June 12 and marching to Central Park amazed at the breadth of the rally's appeal – from babies in backpacks to greatgrandmothers, there were people there from all walks of life, over a million from around the world. I remember thinking: How can I tie into this great sea of energy, become a lasting part of it, contribute my energy to it? Returning on the bus, I met a young woman from Random House who asked, "How would you like us to send you a copy of a book we've just published?" Sure, I said. About three weeks later Jonathan Schell's *Fate of the Earth* arrived. I read it in three nights, a chapter each night, and its impact on me was tremendous. Schell states that the most astonishing single fact about the arms race is that everybody just accepts it. He admonishes us to stop "business as usual" until the "monster" is brought under control. All else is secondary. I took this as a personal challenge. Given the enormity of the problem, I wondered how to proceed, how to make my contribution. Over the years I had seen myself, friends and others involved in civil rights, Vietnam and other social issues, swallowed up in the vastness, the scale, of the problem, become burned out and end up despairing.

One day I thought that maybe the best way for me to deal with the situation was to be very specific, and to use my specific skills. I had been a photographer for about fifteen years, trained and working in the classical tradition. In recent years I had begun adding interviews of my subjects, as if in accompaniment to the pictures. For me photography always has been, to use Edward Weston's visionary phrase, "a voyage of discovery" – to find, to reveal. Now, with interviews I sought to explore another dimension: to listen, to hear, to understand.

Two truly special friends, John Giannini and Kathy Huston, each in their own way, suggested that if I could somehow connect my skills with my concerns for peace the result could be very powerful. The form occurred to me: I would go find those who had been in New York on June 12, or their counterparts; I would search out, interview and photograph those actively working for peace. This would be my contribution.

Once the form was clear in my mind, I knew I could only approach the work as an artist, which for me meant not knowing where the action would take me. At this point I formulated two self-imposed rules: one, I would not concern myself with peace professionals or members of the clergy, because peace is their business; two, I would stay clear of famous people, preferring instead to go to the grassroots – perhaps to test my faith in democracy and common sense – although I allowed myself exceptions in one or two instances.

What I found was that almost every person I connected with was sustained in large part by his or her own spiritual journey, whether traditional or nontraditional, singular or in community.

With the form clear in mind I began at my home base, Chicago. Luckily, several of the first persons I contacted were very encouraging and referred me to others. Although I didn't realize it immediately, a rudimentary network, a way of working, was emerging. After these initial months in Chicago I was eager to expand my territory, to take the idea on the road. Intuitively, I chose Minneapolis.

Not knowing anyone there, I called my friend Norman Watkins at the CALC office in Chicago to find out if CALC (Clergy and Laity Concerned, a group originally formed in opposition to the war in Vietnam) had an office in Minneapolis. They did have a chapter there, which I contacted. Stating my intention to meet, interview and photograph persons actively working for peace, I asked for referrals.

The day after arriving in Minneapolis I met Mary White, a remarkable woman, a social worker and teacher of social work who chooses not to follow old forms. Rather, she uses her skills and knowledge in empowerment of herself and others; she teaches others to then teach yet others –

a kind of living tree, a continuously growing network. I believe I learned more during the forty-five-minute interview with Mary White than in any other forty-five minutes of my life. I came to appreciate the intricacy and simplicity of process and, by listening more, came to think of the best interviews as music – a connection, flowing and improvisational dialogue.

After about ten days in Minneapolis I returned to Chicago, where I developed my film, and made contact sheets and a few work prints. I took the prints to the Peace Museum and showed them to the director, Mark Rogovin. I had volunteered at the museum and knew he understood photography, both from his own background as an artist and muralist and from his exposure to photography as an art form through his father, Milton Rogovin, the wonderful photographer in Buffalo, New York. Mark liked the work but urged me to expand its scope.

Expand it I did. A journey of nine months took me more than thirty thousand miles, through thirty-eight states, to the four corners of the country, in a crisscross pattern marked by occasional returns to home base to develop my film and think through what was unfolding. I interviewed and photographed approximately two hundred persons from all walks of life. My main focus was on personal transformation – how people awaken and what they do next. The concerns of those I met ranged from doing something good for their body, in order to be growing in greatness, to achieving complete and total world disarmament, and many points in between.

How did I find these people? Through a simple combination of trusting my intuition, basic networking, personal reference and luck. Soon the problem of finding far too many prospects arose. Heading for Tulsa, for example, with the name of a person to contact, I would typically call ahead, asking if the individual would be available and if he or she would see if others might be available also. Invariably my contact would proudly present me with a list eight to ten people I "must" see. The task, given the constraints of time and the vastness of this country, became how to decide graciously which two or three to contact.

I met doctors and ranchers, homemakers and shopkeepers, lawyers and warehousemen, scientists, medicine men, veterans and students. I met them in their yards and fields, in their kitchens and living rooms, in their foundries and offices. I was continually struck by how different each individual's story was, while at the same time all in a commonality of purpose: making peace.

I preferred doing the interview first and came to it with very few questions already in mind. As I said, I focused on personal awakening, what people did with it, and how they sustained themselves in the long run. My only specific questions were inquiries about fears and hopes. Without exception, I found that the interviews established a rapport, a feeling tone, transferable into making the photograph. (I use the word "making" here deliberately, as contrasted with "taking", not only for its less expropriative connotation, but to affirm the work involved in the entire photographic process.)

I then asked the person where we should do his or her picture, and who he or she wanted to include in it. I always thought of the entire event as a collaboration. Usually they preferred their home or workplace. Considerations of time, light and location had a bearing, but I did not let these factors control the situation. It was to flow freely.

Learning to pace myself was important. In the beginning I was so excited with this method that I pursued it with almost maniacal urgency and vigor, feeling a great fire within me. Propelled as well by Schell's admonition, I found myself traveling with great energy, intensity and zeal. Many days in Minneapolis I worked from 10:00 a.m. until 2:00 a.m. with hardly a break. Only far into the project did I learn to slow down a bit. In retrospect, I wish I had spent more time – more relaxed time – with those I met. But while doing the work I was powerfully driven, often thinking to myself, "If I don't do this, no one else will." What did I find out? What did I learn? Besides gaining personal empowerment, those working for peace need to feel more connected to one another. Whether in Tupelo, Mississippi, or Sheridan, Wyoming, where the peace community may consist of two or three persons, or in Boston or San Francisco, where the numbers are in the thousands, individuals and organizations need to be connected, they need to encourage each other. The cause is better served by more connections.

Peace and justice are inseparable, and anyone who truly realizes this must inevitably ask questions about the American lifestyle. A society that promotes and consumes outrageous luxuries can easily believe that it needs outrageous weaponry to protect itself. We need go no farther than our local supermarkets to begin questioning why bananas shipped from Guatemala and Honduras cost less than apples grown in our own home states. Are we really to believe that "Juan and Juanita" are happy harvesting export crops for us, while half of their own children die of malnutrition and dysentery before the age of five? As Alia Johnson in Berkeley, California, so cogently realizes, it is not a coincidence that we have nuclear weapons, and Guatemalans work for us for thirty cents a day.

The effects of our war-machine economy cannot be underestimated. World-wide military spending now amounts to more than $2.5 billion a day. Such expenditure not only inhibits economic development and environmental enhancement, but, in fact, leaves few resources for anything beyond the arms race itself; the true cost of the arms race is in what might have been. Our own Department of Defense has contracts in every state, and those provide jobs which are much sought after because they pay very well. As Chuck Guenther in St. Louis so clearly observes: "I used to think of the defense industry as middle class welfare: now I consider it organized crime." I found that those working on peace issues are overwhelmingly white, middle and upper-middle class (although there are heroic exceptions). As an American Indian woman in Minneapolis, who had pulled herself up from welfare mother to mayoral assistant, said: "When you get up in the morning and your choice is between tennis shoes for the kids and toilet paper, you don't think about world peace." This inequity must be confronted so that all may become involved in the peace movement.

Most crucially, I found that people need to believe in themselves and to feel their power and their value. Peace starts with the individual, with me and you. The military-industrial complex will resist change, as it stands to profit from the arms race. People must be bold. Strong.

We cannot all be a Martin Luther King, but each of us *can be* a Rosa Parks. We need to find the good, the peace that already exists, and celebrate that. Celebrate the peacemaking that continues in our lives – the simple human dramas – every day, hundreds of times each day.

On this journey I was constantly amazed at the tremendous courage of those I encountered. I hope that others find courage in their examples, awaken and transform their own lives: often it doesn't take much. This is my hope for my contribution.

I have come to believe that it only takes a few brave persons to set these good forces in motion. As Stephen Mershon, a young family lawyer in Louisville, so poignantly states: "At some point in time, somebody's gotta be brave enough to say, well, they killed my brother; I'm not going to go back there and kill their brother. I'm going to go back with an olive branch and say, I lost my brother, I know how important your brother is to you. Let's start talking."

I think what we need today, more than anything, is imagination. Imagine what a world without weapons would be like. Imagine what could be done with that $2.5 billion per day. Imagine just a small fraction of that $2.5 billion – say, one one-thousandth of it, just $2.5 million – coming to your town, right into your neighborhood. Imagine $2.5 billion in affordable housing for young couples just starting out, in improved health care, new hope for the elderly. Imagine that bridge you cross everyday on the way to work. Imagine that bridge rebuilt, made safe again. How good is *your* "national security" if that bridge collapses tomorrow evening?

I think what we need today is not more data that we can't deal with. We need a few lines of poetry – not thicker skins, but more open hearts. As Langston Hughes reminds us:

> *Hold fast to dreams*
> *For when dreams go*
> *Life is a barren field*
> *Frozen with snow.*

Noreen Warnock

Originally from Lima, Ohio, artist Noreen Warnock lives with her family in an average, working class neighborhood on Chicago's North Side.

1

After Gavin was born – I think he was a little over a year old – I started waking up in the middle of the night, four nights in a row. It was incredibly intense. All I would think about was how I was the mother of a son, and the world was in this situation. I think with him being a boy I was really more afraid. The way our system is now, the idea of him having to go into some sort of military service . . . I just started thinking about it a lot. I'd wake up and would get up – it was three or four in the morning – and I actually came out here to the counter and stood here and said "What can I do? I have to do something."

I would stand at this counter, and I would just stare out these windows. Sometimes I would come over and open the windows. I could see the world out there and was really feeling this. I can't connect it to anything that was happening in the news. It just seemed like all of a sudden I was waking up.

Then, right out of the blue, I got a phone call the fifth day, and this woman said, "Noreen, have you ever heard of a group called Women for Peace?" "No, but it sounds perfect. Who are they and where are they, and what is it you have in mind?" She said that there was some kind of a fundraiser for the group at a church, and she wondered if Jim and I were interested in going with her and her husband. So we went, and I was impressed enough that I took a flyer home with me. Later I called the office, and they sent me another flyer with a list on the back that you could check off, a list of what you were interested in doing. It was sort of intimidating because there were so many things that needed to be done. There were so many things they needed help with.

The thing about this particular group that I like is that it's been around for twenty-one years; it has a lot of history. A lot of times you go into a group and everything seems to have this hierarchy and you feel like you're never going to be able to really do anything. But this wasn't like that. I had the feeling that they were just very open to any new person's ideas and feelings and reached out in a nice kind of way. Right away there were things for me to do. Any ideas you have, anything you want to do, pretty much you just do it. Sometimes it kind of gets chaotic and at loose ends, but in other ways it's really wonderful because people who have an idea, who really want to pursue it, can just go to it.

Six months after this interview, Noreen, through Women for Peace, organized and chaired the Mother's Day Peace March in Chicago. Over 10,000 people participated.

Mary White

Mary White, social worker and teacher of social work, is the mother of four sons and a daughter. She lives with her family on the south side of Minneapolis in the same neighborhood in which she grew up.

2

I got a phone call from Marian Hamilton in October of last year. She said she and her friend Polly Mann had had dinner and decided that something had to be done about the kinds of priorities our country seemed to be going more and more into. It was a kind of madness. Polly Mann was the one that thought of the name. She said, "I've got a name for an organization. Women Against Military Madness, and the initials are WAMM – terrific. Now all we need is an organization to go with the name."

I can remember how the name first affected me. I thought, That sounds kind of frightening. But I thought, OK, it's a good name, it's strong. I tried it out on my family and a few friends, and it was very controversial. People said, "You should have a name that suggests you're for peace." And I said, "Well, it's a good point, except that everyone is for peace, and right now we're at a stage where we're protesting to survive. So we need a strong name." And the more I tried to discuss my feelings about it, the more invested I got in the name and became very comfortable with it. But at first it was startling.

I wasn't very aware of the nuclear arms race a year ago. I was aware of it, but when I look back, I think I was in a state of denying it as so many of us are: It's a big problem, I don't know anything about it, and somebody will take care of it. Or if they don't there's nothing I can do about it. Sort of drawing the curtain.

I think just meeting with these women and talking about things that I was very interested in – like what was happening in the military budget and how it was affecting social programs which I'm involved with as a social worker – that was a real important factor for me. I think the whole question for our country, which has so much in terms of natural riches and resources and gifts, should be: What are we doing with these?

Instead of using these for the betterment of humankind, we are using so much of our resources for military power. Putting it into death rather than life. Our assistance to other countries – it's military aid, number one. Other things are secondary. I began seeing the connections between our economic, corporate way of life and protection of the military-industrial complex.

It was like, my God, once I opened my mind to it it was like, this is too much.

I think when I was allowed to feel I was connected with something that *could* make a difference, not *maybe* make a difference, that a significant change happened for me. Connecting with some other people who are interested; the support, the lifeline. That I could then allow myself to open up to these feelings, because otherwise, what can you do with them if you're all alone? You have to almost go back to denial as a defense to survive. And it was like allowing me to work through feeling so depressed and hopeless and getting angry. I think anger is real good. It gives you that adrenalin to get going. I think it was a real important thing to find that support from other women. And then with them to help develop actions that could express how we felt. It was sort of like different stages. But I don't think you work through these stages completely, because the issue is not resolved.

It feels right. It just feels good. It feels like you're . . . and so the doubts about what I'm doing are gone. I know it's right. Daniel Berrigan had a wonderful statement in the movie *In the King of Prussia*, when he was on the stand. It's excellent, it expresses so much. He said, "I cannot not do what must be done." He doesn't really want to go to jail. It's frightening and scary, and it's painful, and there's loss in other areas of your life. But you do it because you cannot not do it.

It's like we're being pulled into it because it has to be done. Somebody has to take the responsibility. And I think that's a key phrase in the empowerment process: *individual responsibility*. That's what we're trying to help ourselves find, so we can help others find it as well. And so it's a learning process.

You need to plunge yourself into it and realize that it's real empowering to know you can learn the names of those weapons amd learn how much they cost. And that's another part of why empowerment is especially exciting for women. Because it's empowering us in other areas of life as well. If I can get up and give a speech on the military budget, which I never thought I'd be able to, that's really empowering. It's having to learn, having to read and learn first, what the facts are and then using them in public speaking. And I probably never would have done that except that I feel so committed to this issue at WAMM. If you have an idea, you do it. Because there's nobody else that's going to be able to do it. Everyone is working right up to their limit, and so it's not the kind of group where you can sit around and say that's a wonderful idea and a big committee plans it and the most talented person is the public speaker.

What we try to do to structure this process is to use small groups of women. We train facilitators to work with small groups of friends or people at work, or people in their church or their neighborhood. They are support and action groups. Part of this is education, because we find the best way to get educated is as we go along, rather than setting a period of time that we're going to study and educate ourselves and then we'll act a year later. We kind of do it all at once. And it's been wonderful. The creative process works. We've come up with much more imaginative things than we could ever begin to think of.

We urge women to fit it into their daily lives at work, or whatever. That's the key point we stress. Help people fit it into daily lives, weave it into their daily lives. We give examples of things people can do. Start a conversation chain. Talk to one person about the issue every day. Read an article a day; educate yourself. Don't try to take it all on at once. Just once a day, there's something in every newspaper about it. Wear a WAMM button and maybe sell another. Talk to your family. Empower the people around you about the issue. Take it to your workplace, to your churches, to your meetings. Connect it with other issues. If people are saying, "Oh, food prices are so high," connect it with inflation and the military budget. All these connections can be made. It will mushroom and grow.

Mary Swenson

Born and raised in Mendota Village, a small town of three hundred, ten miles from downtown St. Paul, Mary lives in a large shared household in Minneapolis, where she works for systemic change in food distribution with the Hunger Action Coalition, and where she's active in the Honeywell Project, an ongoing protest concerned with conversion of Honeywell's defense contracts to peaceable products and services. An advocate of consciously simplified lifestyle, Mary recently celebrated the seventh anniversary of "no car," opting instead for a bicycle and "the bus."

3

I come from the oldest town in the state of Minnesota, Mendota Village. It's an Indian word that means meeting of the waters, and it's where the Minnesota River and the Mississippi River come together. The oldest church in the state is there, the first governor's home, and it's only ten miles from downtown St. Paul. I bike out there in the summertime almost every Sunday to see my family.

So I'm from a small town, about three hundred people. They've got real deep roots. My mother's lived on the same plot of land for fifty-six years. Everybody knows everybody, and everybody knows everybody's cat and dog. And whenever I want to catch up on what's going on, I just stop at the post office and talk to Rita. I enjoy it. I'm glad I grew up there.

At the University of Minnesota, I started in biology but graduated in child psychology. This was during the Vietnam War, and coming from Mendota Village it was quite a shock to find all these people protesting in the streets and against classes. And I was totally overwhelmed by the number of people going to the same place to get an education. It took me about two years to realize what was going on. I would listen to different speakers and all. But all of a sudden, I started looking at things differently, and started joining the protest movement against the war. It made me feel hopeful.

I work with the Hunger Action Coalition. We exist to educate people about the underlying causes of hunger. We're funded by the major church denominations, and we work mostly within churches, but we're also available to public school systems and other nonchurch organizations. Basically what we do is act as a resouce center for educating about hunger, and that includes militarism and hunger and budget transfers from social service programs, Food Stamps and AFDC into the military. And U.S. lifestyle. We have a speakers' bureau and audiovisuals that we send out to colleges and churches.

We ask people to look at our lifestyle; with 6 percent of the world's population, we consume 40 percent of the world's nonrenewable resources. This relates to hunger in a number of different ways. Use of scarce fuels here for frivolous reasons causes the price of fuel to go up all over the world, and people in developing countries cannot afford to use the fuel to transport their food. Another cause is land distribution in Third World countries, where overall, 3 percent of the population controls over 80 percent of the agricultural land.

Right here in Minnesota, this great agricultural state, we only produce 25 percent of the food we eat. Our corn goes to feed cattle, our soybeans into industrial products. The problem is in who decides what is grown. It's not a problem of production. It's a problem of power. Those in power make decisions about what is most profitable to grow. It takes about eight pounds of grain to produce one pound of beef, so eating meat is high up on the food chain.

I've had the opportunity to do a study in Guatemala and Honduras for the Third World Institute. We visited places – beautiful, grassy hillsides – where you see a fenced-in area where cattle are being grown. And yet the people are starving, and that cattle gets exported.

We saw hopeful signs, too. In Guatemala we visited a co-op in which World Neighbors, an organization here, had helped sixty-four landless peasant families acquire small parcels for the first time since 1500, when they had lost it to the Spanish.

Instead of being stuck for the rest of their lives picking coffee for a dollar a day, these sixty-four families had contoured their land and were growing corn, beans and squash, which had been their ancestors' diet, the ancient Mayans. It was just uplifting and inspiring to see what people can do once they had the chance to make the decisions about what was going to be grown. They chose to grow food to feed their own families first.

The tragic part of this wonderful story is that the co-op was seen as a threat to the status quo. The people who owned the coffee plantation saw this as a real dangerous thing to have as a model. People were talking about it. We heard that a year ago last August, the military came into the co-op and beheaded twenty of the men.

It makes me furious that here it is, our tax monies, going to support that kind of repression in Central America. It makes me mad! I think anger can be used to really give you energy to turn around and say, What can I do to stop this?

Right here in Minneapolis is the corporate headquarters of Honeywell. Honeywell does about a billion dollars a year of weapons production, including parts for the Trident submarine, the Polaris submarine, the B-52 bomber, the F-111 fighter, ICBMs, Minutemen ICBMs, etc. And so I'm with the Honeywell Project, which has chosen to work on trying to get nuclear weapons production and weapons production in general stopped in Minnesota.

The Honeywell Project has been ongoing for years. We don't give up. Just this month, November 4 and 5, we had a large demonstration, about five hundred people on Thursday the fourth, to demonstrate against Honeywell's involvement in the production of nuclear weapons systems and also cluster bombs. The first day was basically a demonstration. The second day, thirty-six of us did civil disobedience by blocking all of the entries to the corporation's headquarters.

We have these little victories, and it gives you a whole lot of energy. I feel very much alive by all this. It gives me direction, a sense of purpose. I am encouraged.

My brother is a truck driver for a beer distributor here in the Twin Cities, and the man who drives the truck with him said to him, Hey did you hear what happened at Honeywell this morning? And my brother says, Hear about it! My sister got arrested. And the guy says, Yeah? Well you tell her next time they do that I'll be sittin' right next to her. So I thought, here is someone who works driving a truck, is a union member and feels strongly about this. That's great. And my mother is a waitress, and she confided in her friends who are also waitresses the day I was arrested, and they all got together and called the Honeywell Project office and said that if anyone needed bail they'd post it. So I thought, here were women who for the most part are having financial problems on their own and yet are committed and willing to do that.

It made me feel very proud I'd come from there.

Priscilla Humay-Louis

Lake Forest, Illinois, long the enclave of Chicago's gentry, and considered by many lifelong residents as impossible to organize, is the home of Priscilla Humay-Louis. Successful artist and mother of four, she practically single-handedly initiated Lake Forest-Lake Bluff Concerned Citizens for Peace.

4

I started myself. I rented a room in a neighborhood community center. I started compiling names in January or February of last year, until May. I compiled as much as I could, and I started calling around asking: Is there a peace group here? I kept asking. I had no idea what was going on. I tried finding out.

It was in the back of my mind for a very long time. My husband is a doctor. Reading the information accounts of A-tests in Utah, things that are continuously covered up, you realize something is happening that's pretty awful. You get a gut feeling. Sometimes you can work on a gut feeling because maybe that's the only true thing that comes across.

Something's brewing somewhere and it doesn't smell too good – that's the feeling.

For at least a year and a half to two years, I thought, Well, it doesn't look like we're going in a very safe direction. Somehow or other the word *war* kept drifting in. And I thought, My God, I don't even know about war. I can remember being in school, one of the Catholic schools in Chicago, and hiding under my desk. We're having an air raid drill. Well, what good would the desk do? When you grow up with that kind of thing, you think, It's been with me all my life. What an awful, ridiculous thing to have on your back all your life.

I think you feel that you have to do something, and I don't even know what the motivating force is. It could be that I have kids; it could be that I really love the world. I get a big kick out of every little crazy shell, every little crazy thing, every little tree. It's a beautiful world. What are we doing? What in God's name are we doing? Can we continue like this? How many more will we have; how many more are we building up?

When you start looking at different maps and where missiles sit and where other silos sit and where nuclear plants are located, an accident could happen anywhere. That's scary. It's serious. It's very serious. I want my kids to grow up. Why bring them into this world, go through all the pain and agony and having them crying in their wet diapers and everything and then, poof, nothing. Why? It's not fair. It's not fair to a fish in the water. It's not fair to anybody. We're being selfish. And for what? If we blow each other up, who's going to care whether it's communism or capitalism? We're going to be groveling for food, groveling for water. If we're around.

It's frightening. You start thinking about it, and you think, Boy, I wish it were all settled because I'd like to start doing something else. Well, I can't do something else. I'd like to get back to my work, my painting. Every time I start I think, Well, this is ridiculous; so I sell it through a gallery or it's in someone's home or it's in a corporation somewhere, what is the big priority at this point? The most creative thing I can do right now is work towards some sort of peaceable solution to the problems.

It's like a piece of art. Someone comes up to me and says, "How long did it take you to do that?" Or, "When did you stop?" Or, "When did you start doing it?" There is no period of time, because everything you've seen or touched or felt comes out of that, even if you were two years old or ten years old or earlier. And it will continue for a whole lifetime. It doesn't stop. That's how I think you have to view these things. There may be times when you may get a little down, times when sympathetic people say they can't come to this meeting, or that, but you have to remind yourself, I'm here.

Why do each other in just because we disagree? You work it out, you keep working it out. You don't stop because negotiation fails. Maybe the negotiators don't know enough about Soviet psychology, culture. Maybe we don't know enough about them humanistically to be able to negotiate. Who do we choose for negotiators? Military people? Of course they're going to propagate the military. But if we can really understand the history of the Soviet Union, and they us, that's hopeful.

People celebrate Chanukah; marvelous, learn about it, it's beautiful. Christmas? It's beautiful. So what; so it's different. These are cultural differences, and there are political differences, but I think nations that want to war for an economic goal of some sort make the differences more profane and exaggerated than they actually are. They stress the differences. There really is no big, big difference. Basically, people all want the same thing. All people can intermix and propagate, we are one species.

We had five Japanese visitors to our community center in Lake Forest; they came from the United Nations delegation. We had a potluck supper and a question-answer session with a translator. It was a very enlightening process. They told us, "Please keep telling us: 'Remember Pearl Harbor,' and we will keep telling you: 'Remember Hiroshima and Nagasaki.'" That was the point they made. They said, "Yes, we did a lot of atrocities; yes, we are embarrassed and we're ashamed." Never to forget; to remember. The Holocaust, remember. Remember these things, they're awful. No war's a good war.

Clint Gardner

Both the Norwich (Vermont) Peace Center and the Bridges for Peace project were born in no small part due to Clint Gardner, former Army officer and businessman. Clint has had personal contacts with Russians here, in the Soviet Union and in Europe, since 1945. His active involvement with the United Church of Christ, locally and statewide, is another source of his inspiration.

5

My wife and I have been importers, and still are, of handicrafts from various countries. Actually, I think we import from some thirty countries all around the world. For about three years, we've been developing the Norwich Center, but we've adopted the name the Norwich Peace Center, to make it clearer what we're doing.

I've been interested and concerned about these issues, particularly the confrontation between the United States and the Soviet Union, since the Second World War. As the war was ending, I left my artillery outfit, where I was a first lieutenant in an artillery combat battalion, and volunteered for military government. And within six or eight weeks after doing that–this was in the spring of '45–I found myself in command of Buchenwald, the concentration camp, two days after they'd liberated it. It was an experience that sort of shook up an American who was so used to not being invaded or bombed or having anything catastrophic happen to us. The first news that people had been exterminated by the millions in gas chambers was borne in upon us as we arrived. We met many who had managed to escape from Auschwitz one way or the other.

I went on to Berlin and was managing editor of the newspaper published by the military government in 1948. That was when the Russians surrounded Berlin and told us there would be no way of getting to Berlin, and we could jolly well leave. We preferred not to leave since that might have begun unraveling the whole postwar situation in Europe. So we, as is well known, had an airlift. My first son was born in Berlin, and his milk was flown in from Denmark.

This tension between East and West–I experienced there, on the receiving end of the Russian intransigence. But all the time I was well aware, or thought I was properly aware, that it was not a one-sided thing. Sometimes the Russians were pushing people around; other times we were throwing our weight around. It struck me that it was very unlikely that we would avoid a third world war, which would probably be an end to the world. Very much what I'd experienced at Buchenwald on a small scale–the extermination of peoples. Samuel Pesaw, who is now an international lawyer and a survivor of Auschwitz, in a talk I heard recently in Cambridge, referred to the extermination camps as a dress rehearsal for nuclear holocaust.

It is my sense that the human race is capable of these things. We Americans don't quite realize, because of our protection by oceans, how much the rest of the world feels the pain. Particularly the Russians, who lost twenty million in the Second World War. I'm well aware that I as a soldier probably survived only because the Russians had something like four or five times as many divisions of Germans fighting against them on the Eastern Front.

They were absorbing most of the fighting, and they're well aware of this. They have always felt that after the Second World War they had as much right as any country to participate in the peace and create the world that would come out of that. To a large extent, they felt that the United States and the Western countries tried to prevent them from playing a constructive role, which I think has put them into their frequently negative position. Had they been accepted as a legitimate country after the Revolution, to say nothing of after the Second World War, the whole development might well have been different. Had we not begun to threaten them and they us, the peacemaking could have begun then, and it didn't.

That was why I began to learn Russian history and language. I studied at the University of Paris and thought after this tour in Berlin I might stay in the State Department and pursue studies in that field. But I didn't, and my first visit to Russia was actually as an importer when I went there in '78 to buy handicrafts. Since that time, while working on the development of the Norwich Peace Center, I've had sort of a two-pronged interest. Many of my friends who've been concerned about the deterioration of our relations with the Russians have helped me form a project, sponsored by the United Church of Christ in Vermont and New Hampshire, called Bridges for Peace. The Norwich Center serves as the base for that project, an office and a place where you can receive mail.

I'm a commissioned worker for the United Church of Christ, as a peace worker, and have delivered some talks from a spiritual perspective within churches. The spiritual dimension has become increasingly clear to me: the Russians are very much part of a strong Christian tradition, perhaps more than they are products of the Marxist-Leninist revolution. I think Russians really know this, but can't admit it formally.

I sense, talking with Russians when I was there, and talking with a few who visited this country, that they feel very deeply a responsibility for the fate of the earth, as Jonathan Schell has put it. The spiritual dimension is felt by them, whether they be communists or not. They realize with a sense of awe that they and we may be responsible for destroying each other, completely obliterating each other, all the Northern Hemisphere, perhaps the whole planet, and beginning the unraveling of history. We live in a time of great peril for both of us, and something approaching a miracle has to occur to undo this headlong race to destruction. The poignancy here is, I think the Christian tradition in both countries may provide the way out.

A Russian communist we invited up to the Norwich Center just a month ago, who is a correspondent for the *Literary Gazette* in this country and had never visited New England, asked a friend of mine whether he might do so. We extended him an invitation under the Bridges for Peace project, and he was here. His name is Anatoly Manakov, and he's about forty.

Anatoly came up here for three days in mid-October. He indicated that he was a Communist Party member, had come up in that tradition, that side of Russian life. He said, "Of course, you know, I am baptized." He also actually asked if he might go to the church service. I had thought it would be embarrassing. My wife and I thought, Well, we don't want to inflict that on him while he's here. He knew that the project, Bridges for Peace, was church-sponsored, but I didn't want to involve him in it too much.

We're hoping to have some Orthodox priests and perhaps a Baptist minister be in the delegation that comes from the Soviet Union in May, but since Anatoly was just a newspaper correspondent, I didn't think that was the thing to push on him. But he asked to go. So we went to the service, and a hymn book was thrust into our hands, and he joined me in singing the last part of the service. Then we went to the coffee hour afterward, and he enjoyed meeting people there. That evening we had a potluck for him with a large number of members of our church joining and asking him questions.

I'm afraid that our use of the Russians today as the source of all evil is, again to put this in spiritual dimensions, well known as the trick of the Devil. That is, he is the person, the Devil is the person who makes you feel that all right is on your side, and that somebody else is completely to blame for everything that goes wrong in the world. This business of categorizing the Russians as the source of everything that is evil, all the things that go wrong in the Third World, say El Salvador or wherever, is something that is profoundly dangerous.

I know of nobody who warns us better against it than George Kennan, the dean of Russian specialists in this country. Kennan has reinforced my perspective on this, and I think that of many Americans, by saying that for the last several years, maybe even for a decade or more, Americans have been subjected to a process of the Russians being given an enemy image. He calls this a process of dehumanization of both the people and their leaders.

Interestingly enough, in a recent issue of *Time* – Richard Nixon was being interviewed by *Time's* diplomatic correspondent – Nixon used the word *hope*. He said the Reagan administration was in danger of not presenting any hope for the future. To have Richard Nixon coming back out of his . . . out of a position of having been set aside – and I can't say that my instincts have ever led me to look to him for spiritual guidance – it was interesting that he emphasized that you have to have some vision of the future.

I don't think that hope or faith or love, the great Christian virtues, come automatically, and they're never assured. I don't have hope all the time by any means. But I think that in the Christian tradition we are very much instructed not to give up. The sin against the Holy Spirit, which is considered the primary sin in Christian teaching, is cynicism – giving up on the human project.

I get my hope out of a strong sense that our heritage can't be given up, that we can't give up on the project of the human race, and that we're very close to doing that if we don't turn around. We can't allow history to pursue its inexorable course. I think one great sign of hope is the depth and what I believe is a sustained effort on the part of broad sections of American society to stay with this and not have it a flash in the pan.

Alice Emmons

Born and brought up in Springfield, Vermont, a town of ten thousand noted for its precision tool industry, Alice Emmons lives cooperatively at Whitcombe Farm, "up the hill, at the end of the pavement." Long concerned about the environment, and with a degree in plant science, she worked until recently as a secretary in Springfield. Describing herself as a common, ordinary Vermonter, Alice was recently elected to the Vermont legislature from Springfield with the rather refreshing platform: "If you vote for me, just promise that you'll let me know your concerns."

6

There are four of us who live in this house, a cooperative household. We have a cow, which we derive all our dairy products from: our own butter, our own cheese, our own yogurt. We have hens, and this past summer we had some turkeys. Last year one of my housemates had a pig. And then we have a very large garden, so that we're basically self-sufficient in terms of food.

My dad came from . . . both my parents were born in Vermont, and the background has been farming, agriculture. My mother lived on a farm before she moved here to Springfield. And then my dad worked in one of the machine tool shops in Springfield, but I was influenced by the farms around. We had farms right over the hill.

I also think my parents very much influenced my life by their way of life. They're in their seventies now, so I was brought up – I always resented it – "oh, you're so old-fashioned," but they taught me some values. Back in the fifties and sixties, we were heating with wood. That was our way of life. We had a kitchen wood stove, cook range, and we still have it. My parents still use it. We did all our canning and made bread, and we kept on to those old ways.

Recently I saw a bumper sticker that says, *Vermont, A Way of Life*. And it is. People say Vermonters are slow and backward, but I've lived in other states, and I've always had a yearning to get back to Vermont because the people here *are* different. Vermonters are so in touch with the land. We have to deal with the seasons; we have to deal with summer, which is nice, and we have to deal with winter, which is twenty below and five feet of snow. We know the seasons in the year, and they're like the seasons in our life. When you have to deal with weather so directly, I think it toughens you up, and it's awareness, an awareness of life.

One time I was living in Massachusetts, and this person was giving me directions to Lawrence and telling me what interstate to get on, and I said, "Well, is that north or south or east or west?" She said, "Good heavens, don't ask me that. I wouldn't know anything about that." But that's the way we live. You go east for this and you go north for that. It's because we have to deal with the changing seasons. We have to deal with a changing life. I think that just keeps us more in tune with how everything is interconnected. It's true in my life.

I've always been environmentally, biologically minded. When I was going to the University of New Hampshire in the mid-seventies, Seabrook was being built, the beginning of it. There was an issue concerning the marshland, the design of cooling towers, and the hot water being emitted into the backwaters of the ocean – a whole environmental issue. Out of that came my awareness of nuclear weapons back in about 1976, 1978.

About August of '81 I moved back to Springfield, and I found there was a small peace group organizing around the town meeting nuclear arms freeze vote for '82. I started going to the meetings, but at first I thought, This is kind of off the wall. What difference does it make, voting for this at town meeting? Then I got more into it, and I was elected chairperson of the group. That just added fuel to the fire, and it just kept going and going and going.

When I first stated, I was working in one of the machine tool shops in town. I was a secretary. We had to go around and get signatures on a petition so that we could have this resolution on the ballot. I was petrified to go to my coworkers, to go out to get signatures on this petition from people who were working in the shops. Because they use as an argument that it's jobs. But it isn't jobs! We're not getting any jobs from the nuclear industry, not up here we're not! And so one day at work I was just sitting there with those petitions. I was petrified. These were people I'd been working with for about eight months, grown up with, graduated with their kids. One day, I said, "Damn it, I'm going to get out there and start getting some signatures." And I went to about everyone I knew, and in one day I got about forty to fifty signatures.

I just sat down and said, "Well, if I don't do it – this is more patriotic than sitting back and doing nothing." I want to live. I'm proud of the United States, and I want us to continue to be free. And the only way we're going to be free is to have a freeze on nuclear armaments. If not dismantling. So then I started going around, and I said, "This is what we want to put on the town meeting ballot. You don't have to agree with this, you can disagree, all we need is 350 signatures, and if it is on the ballot, then you can vote in privacy how you feel about it." With that approach, people were more than willing to sign. Then the common response was, "Well, I wish they were doing this in Russia," and, "What about the Russians?"

I'd say, "Well, the Russians are human beings like you and I; they have feelings like you and I." And I said, "We have the freedom to do this, we have the freedom to speak out, and that's why I'm doing it." Then one day, right before the vote, right before town meeting, there was one man who was very very conservative, who worked in the next department. He brought in some newspaper articles about the Russians. You can't trust them, and they're the ones who want us to put this freeze movement in the States as a way of undermining our own country. This man really believed this. I had other information, too: I had a newspaper, and I brought that in, and I said, "Well, just read this." And he did. He read it. And later on, he came back and said, "I read everything you gave me, Alice, but I just don't believe it. I want my freedom in this country, and the only way we're going to have our freedom is to build up nuclear arms." I went back to my desk, and I remembered that two people in our group had purchased the film *The Last Epidemic*, and I was thinking, Oh, if he could only see that film and realize that we don't have any freedom *with* nuclear weapons. Then I just started crying, because it really hit me that this man put so much faith in nuclear weapons, and he didn't know the destruction side of it. He just took it for granted that the roads would be there, the utilities would be there, the hospital would be there, the doctors, the nurses, the medicine, everything would be there. They're not going to be there. But he just couldn't see that. It saddened me, it really saddened me.

The night of town meeting I had a feeling the freeze resolution was going to pass in Springfield. I had a feeling it was going to pass in most of the towns in the state, but Springfield was my major focus. That night, the results were 2,121 in favor and 661 opposed—it had passed by a three-to-one margin. I was on cloud nine that whole night.

The next day when I went in to work, people looked at me in a whole different light. Like, oh, she knew something we didn't. It was so funny. And this man who I'd given the literature to came over and said, "Well, you won, didn't you." I said, "No, I didn't win. We all won." I think of that night many, many times.

I think of the night before town meeting, where the people came to the high school and discussed every article on the warrant. Ours was next to last. When it came up, there were four of us in the peace group sitting there side by side, and we just kind of looked at each other. We're not going to say a word; we'll let some other people in town stand up. And there was one man, a retired foreign service officer. He got up and gave such a moving speech. He said, "I have never spoken at a town meeting before in my life, and I have been here seven years. But I feel moved and compelled to say something on this issue. I feel it's a proper place for us to be voting on this in a town meeting because it affects our lives, and I'm in favor of this." He went on and on, why we should vote for it. After that, the head of our school board, a dentist here in town, got out and spoke in favor of the resolution. And a few other people spoke in favor of it. It was so moving.

Afterwards we just kind of sat there and looked at each other and said, "Whew, are we glad we didn't have to say anything." Because we didn't want to be seen just as a peace group saying something; we wanted it to come from the community. And it did. It was a spontaneous response from the community.

I think people are feeling good and feeling OK that they can work for peace. People are feeling it's all right to work for peace instead of war. I feel anger, and I feel frustration when I hear President Reagan saying the American people are communist dupes. I really resent that. Because I saw who voted for this freeze in the town meetings. I'm frustrated because the president just isn't listening to us. And when I hear him saying things like this, I think it's because he's scared, he's very scared. During his presentation on the MX missile, it galled me to hear him say these are peacekeepers. I was almost sick. I said, I can't believe this man honestly believes that.

I have many days of desperation. I think a lot of hope comes from the people I work with, the people I know. And it seems like every day it's growing. People are becoming more aware of the arms race. People everywhere. Somehow you just get out of bed and keep going.

Jim Levinson

Beneficiary of privilege and wealth, bearer of achievement and rank, Jim Levinson lives with his wife, Louise Cochran, and children, Mira, twelve, and Noah, two, at Haley House, a Catholic Worker House on Dartmouth Street in Boston's South End. Here they help feed neighborhood people from a soup kitchen in the basement. And it is here that they chose a life of intentional material proverty, while their spiritual richness unfolds daily. Jim's musical gifts are an added delight and inspiration.

7

I lived in India for six years, and Louise and I together in Bangladesh for two years, and in addition, I spent lots of time, shorter visits, working in Indonesia and Thailand, Pakistan, Sri Lanka and the Philippines, working on international food and nutrition. Most of this with the U.S. government, and when it wasn't the U.S. government it was another fancy large-scale bureaucratic agency, UN agencies or the World Bank. And I did that all told for eighteen years, including the time that I spent teaching there. I spent four years teaching international nutrition at MIT, and international nutrition planning programs, which I was invited to set up and direct. I spent a lot of time doing music, and that's been very much a thread that's gone through all the things that I've done. I've enjoyed that very much. You can be let down by the U.S. Department of Agriculture, but Bach somehow always comes through.

Over these years that I was working in international food and nutrition with these prestigious organizations, it became clear to me that there is an inverse relationship between one's status, prestige, income, reputation and how close one is to the problem. In other words, if one is feeding the hungry child, one is at the bottom of the heap. In terms of status, prestige, income, jobs, being invited to the prestigious conferences, being invited to write journal articles, etc.

If you're training people, you're a notch up. If you're administering a program, you're several notches up, even though you may not see the hungry. And if you're doing what I was doing, which was largely conceptualizing, preparing the theory, doing the planning, writing the journal articles, then indeed, perhaps you never see the poor at all. Then one is at the top. And there is a professional elite of which I was a part, which is very well rewarded for work in hunger. To the point where one can indeed live very well, remarkably well, doing hunger work without being hungry, let alone even seeing the hungry.

I was struck by . . . as a reflection of how outlandish this can become, I was last year offered a position that was to head the division of one of the international agencies that is supposed to be directly involved with malnutrition and the alleviation of hunger. It is located in a place far from hunger, and when I indicated my disinterest in the position, the assumption by the young man that was offering it was that I needed more of a financial incentive, and he told me that the salary that goes with this job – $60,000 a year – is tax free. And that the present incumbent of this job has a villa out on the ocean. Somehow it says a lot, and it's sad.

Sometimes we have experiences that we only begin to understand years later. In my case, there was a very powerful experience I went through about a dozen years ago which was that I surely thought of myself as a good and decent person. I was doing good work; I had been working for the State Department in India. I felt like at that point I was doing something just short of saving the world. It was a little of the mentality that Halberstam writes about in *The Best and the Brightest*. Incredible presumptuousness and cockiness that we had. There's no problem we can't solve as long as we just put together the best minds and go at it systematically, bring to bear the appropriate technology, and away we go. We'll be done. If we need to send five thousand farmers over to India to show them how to farm, let's just do it. Whatever the problem there's got to be a solution; we can do it. And I think it was that kind of mentality that really got us, as Halberstam suggests, into the mess in Vietnam. Coming from that and feeling very cocky and presumptuous, I came back to the States for more graduate study.

At that time I learned that my family, which has a corporation in Pittsburgh, had begun – this was the Vietnam War – had accepted a defense contract for the manufacture of shells. I don't know a great deal about how much that company produced, except that there was until last year in my home a lamp that had a little plaque on it indicating that this shell from which the lamp was made was the one millionth shell turned out by this corporation. And that plant operated for several years, and indeed yielded very rich dividends for all of us in the family.

There were a few people in the family who protested, who said that this was wrong. And as I think back on it, it's striking me that those people might have been regarded as the black sheep of the family, the odd people out, the people who didn't dress quite as well, people surely who didn't have very prestigious jobs. Surely they didn't go to Harvard, have a Ph.D. and work for the State Department. And they were not taken very seriously. Those of us who were the seemingly more attractive, well paid, better dressed of the group rallied – if we didn't rally to the defense of the board, we at least were quiet – we didn't upset the apple cart, we didn't do anything embarrassing. In the words of William Sloan Coffin, I was a nice guy, but by no means yet a good man; that kind of acquiescence.

As I came to reexamine that experience, which only took place in the last couple of years, I think it came most poignantly seeing the film *Hearts and Minds*, which just tore me apart. All I could think of, the litany that went through my mind when I saw that film – those children being killed in the Vietnam War – was: I could spend the rest of my life working, trying to meet the needs of children in the Asian countries, and still my life would remain in the minus column because of my acquiescence to making those shells which killed so many of the innocent.

Just after Noah was born, Louise and I found ourselves spending a lot of time thinking about the kind of life we wanted to lead with a child. And as we looked around, we found a large number of friends, relatives, who earlier in their lives had been very committed and active on issues of peace and justice, who had children and stopped doing that. They would build moats around themselves and take the position self-sacrifice is OK for me, but when it comes to my children, I want only the best. One set of cousins joined something called the Toy of the Month Club, and that phrase for us sort of summed up that syndrome. We looked at it, and I must say, every set of parents, ourselves included, felt some level of attractiveness in that kind of paradigm. You want the best for a kid. There is something of a nesting instinct that parents feel when they have kids.

Then we came across the story of Molly Rush, a woman who lives in Pittsburgh, where we both grew up, and we later met Molly. Molly has six children. She had been mildly involved in civil rights and had come to understand what the threat of nuclear war means for her, and particularly for the children. And she felt that it wasn't enough simply to go on making sandwiches for their lunch boxes. She decided it was necessary to do more, and her way of doing more was to join the Berrigans and others in King of Prussia going into the General Electric plant. Personally disarming weapons; saying, Look, there have been no fewer than six thousand meetings between the U.S. and the Soviets on disarmament, and not a single weapon has been disarmed. And somebody's got to start disarming the weapons, however symbolically, because it's right, and because you cannot not do it. So she went ahead and did it, and she did it for her children. That had a mesmerizing effect on us. And we said, "Wow, what a counterweight to the Toy of the Month Club model." What a compelling notion of the way we live for our children. That just had a walloping effect on us.

At the same time, we had been living for a few months since Noah was born as a traditional nuclear family, and found that to be somewhat inadequate and unsettling. And we found that particularly the case when that summer I went to work in Indonesia and the Philippines. We stopped in Israel and visited a family on the way to Indonesia and spent, for the first time, some days on kibbutzim. We were very attracted to the kibbutz. In retrospect, we realized that it wasn't Israel per se that attracted us, that it was the idea of community. There was something about that notion of community, people living together, working together, sharing the child-care, sharing the preparation of food – all of this was also very compelling.

We came back to Boston and actually began phoning people, saying is there such a place, have you ever heard of such a place where people live in community and work for peace? As it then turned out, by meeting Molly Rush we subsequently found ourselves on the mailing list of Jonah House, where Phil Berrigan and Liz McCallister live in Baltimore. Being on that mailing list, we got an invitation, now just a little more than a year ago, to something called the Feast of the Holy Innocents. That's a Catholic feast day that memoralizes the children that were killed by Herod. And the connection there is just all too vivid and poignant. So for several years the Jonah House people have called together peace resistance folks from all up and down the eastern part of the country to come together to live together in community at St. Stephen's Church in Washington, sleeping in sleeping bags in pews and on the altar. It's an Episcopal church. And then going to demonstrate at the Pentagon. They also have wonderful activities set up for children. And so we got this invitation, somehow felt we must go.

A good friend suggested that it might be a mistake. When you go to something like that you're very stirred up, you come back and no one understands. He said go only if you can find people here who are willing to go down with you and will be able to share it when you come back to Boston. So again we began to phone around. Has anyone ever heard of the Feast of the Holy Innocents? Not getting much pickup until we called the local Catholic Connection, which is a group that coordinates a lot of activitism on Central America and the Urban College of Peace. They told us, "Yes, there is a group in Boston called Alanthus, which meets at Haley House, the Boston Catholic Worker House. So we met the folks at Haley House and went down to the Feast of the Holy Innocents. A few people from the house went, and we all went together. Louise, my daughter Mira, and Noah and I participated in those activities and went to the Pentagon with the folks and had what is probably as close to a conversion experience as I have known in my life. On the steps of the Pentagon there was a die-in, and I had never heard of a die-in before. But there were people like myself who were lying on the steps of the Pentagon with blood and ashes poured over them at the sound of a siren, with a woman singing a song about the young child at Hiroshima who was seven years old and will never grow up. Very powerful emotions began to well up inside as I saw this going on.

Then a van from the group pulled up to the steps of the Pentagon, and it became evident that those bodies were to be loaded into the van. Somehow, right at that moment, both Louise and I felt that very strong urge. I had Noah in my backpack, and Louise took Noah off my back while I stepped forward and picked up one of those bodies. Covered with blood and ashes. I got blood and ashes all over my clothes. All I could do was weep, just weep and hold on to this body for dear life as I loaded this person into the van. And I couldn't let go. People were saying, "You've got to move on because we've got more bodies to load into the van." I just couldn't let go. It was such a powerful, gripping moment. And it became clear to me from that point that life would never be quite the same again, that there was born at that moment a commitment. It was something from this point on that I could not not do.

I came back, began working in the soup kitchen, and that was wonderful also. We had spent that December, Louise and I, with a lot of preparations for Christmas, a lot of time and effort buying things for the kids, but it struck us afterwards that the real gift, even for our kids, even besides ourselves, that Christmas was sharing with them the experience of feeding the homeless downstairs, which we did right before Christmas, and then going together to the Pentagon right afterwards.

We moved into the house in May, and it's very touching how we were welcomed. People go so out of their way to make us, as a family, settled in such a way that we continue to live as a family while we are part of this larger family. Very touching to see how, knowing, for example, that Mira, my daughter by my previous marriage, might feel a bit left out, one of the folks in the house built a loft room for her so that she could have her own room in this house. She was just very touched, and she loves being here. Everyone in the house has basically adopted Noah, and everyone has his or her own special gift to bring to him. One fellow in the house plays boats, and someone else plays football, and someone else spends time in the soup kitchen with him. There is a sense of shared stewardship of the child. It's a wonderful way for a child to grow up. Talk about richness.

It's nice to see also how the reverse is true, how he has been able to bring happiness to some of the people in the soup kitchen while we're working down there. How some of the homeless men have taken to him and feel a connection with him. How some of the elderly women really find great joy in being with him.

Michael Affleck

Michael and Beth Affleck deliberately choose to live with their two young children in one of Rochester's poorer neighborhoods—"the bad part of town" by contemporary middle-class standards. It's here that they attempt to build community, at the asphalt-roots level, while remaining mindful of the global community.

8

Beth and I were married in 1975. We're both from upwardly mobile middle class families. My dad's a GE executive, and Beth's dad is an Allied Chemical executive. We were very much in that mold, very conservative, Republican. When we were married, we decided very quickly that I needed to go back to school if I was actually going to support a family. I had received a bachelor's degree, and Beth had received her bachelor's degree.

I got accepted in a program in health education at the State University of New York at Buffalo. I went for a master's in health education, received the degree, and also received a grant to continue work for the American Heart Association, leading to a doctorate. At the same time, Beth got her master's in health education. We were three years married, had those degrees, and I accepted a position at the State University of New York at Cortland and was a professor there in health education, teaching teachers how to teach health. That was my job. Although I had never taught myself, I taught others how to do it.

We bought a home on the nicest street in town. A beautiful home. We had vinyl carpeting, a custom-made dining room set, cocktail parties all the time, vacations in the Caribbean. We had a wonderful, wonderful life, and we found ourselves growing more and more unhappy. Since Beth was a Lutheran at the time, she found great happiness in the Lutheran community, and the minister there was very very kind to us. He started asking us questions relating the Gospel to our lives, and starting probing our unhappiness in relationship to our having made it. I was twenty-eight years old, and we were set up for life. This was very directly the way he put it to me one day. There was a big cemetery across from the church, and we were just looking over the fence one day on a little walk around town, and he asked me if I planned to be buried in that cemetery. He said, "Are you going to die here? Are you going to be buried in that cemetery?" It was quite startling. I didn't know what to make of it.

Beth and I had decided after our first year of teaching we would take a vacation to California. We started in San Francisco and were staying with my sister, and one day decided to cross the bay to Berkeley to see this

radical town. We walked around the campus, and at one point walked into
the Franciscan School of Theology. We happened to meet the dean, and
talked a little while about some of my interests. He invited me to come to
school that fall, to the Franciscan school. I said, "I guess you don't understand my situation; see, I have this job and a house and family. My life is
back in New York."

The next day we showed up on his doorstep again. He was quite surprised to see us, and we asked him if he was serious, and he said, "Yeah,
yeah I'm serious." So we said OK, we'll do it. The next day we made the
phone calls. I called the state university and I quit my job; then I called the
realtor and said sell the house. And we called our family and said that we
were planning to stay in California, that we'd probably be back just to dis-
pose of all the things in the house and pack up and leave.

We had about eight weeks till school started, and we still had a vacation,
so we continued down California and ended up near San Diego, actually
right on the border. We had gone down to hook up with some friends who
had invited us to see what they had been doing. They worked with a project called *Los Niños*, The Children. The people who work with *Los Niños*
do a very simple thing. There are fifty-thousand – more now – at least
fifty-thousand children who are starving to death in Tijuana, the Mexican
city right across the border. They just collect food on the United States
side, drive across the border, and give it to hungry kids. Very simple idea,
and it saves thousands of kids a year from dying.

There are also hundreds of children who live in the garbage dumps.
Some of the kids are by themselves. But there're many families, up to a
hundred families who live in the garbage dump, who rake the garbage off
the trucks as they come in, sort through it for food to eat. That's what they
have for the day. Coming from the life that we had had, never having seen
a poor person to speak of – we had always stayed away from the bad parts
of town – and going into a city where everybody was poor and going to the
garbage dump where they were literally eating the garbage was quite a
shock to us. Devastating. We spent our first day in Tijuana feeding kids,
playing with them, taking care of minor medical problems, things like
that. Near the end of the day, I was walking along the ridge that overlooks
the garbage dump and could see from the ridge the city of San Diego as
well as the garbage dump in the city of Tijuana; I could look across the
border. And I couldn't imagine what it was in the world that was creating
a situation where San Diego, one of our most beautiful cities, could be
located so close to such absolute destitution.

So while I was standing on the ridge in the twilight, it was actually a dawning experience for me. I could see this beautiful bay that San Diego has, and into the bay was coming a nuclear aircraft carrier. Right at that moment. So for the first time in my life, the question crossed my mind that maybe those weapons weren't protecting the free world. Maybe the people in Tijuana are not protected by our weapons, and maybe they're actually deprived of something because we're spending the money on arms. I didn't know whether the question was valid. I was completely ignorant on everything about these issues.

It was really quite a moment, and the image is really remarkable, too, because the dump was always kept on fire. They'd burn the garbage off, so that there are fires that go through that dump, the fires keep wandering through as they keep the garbage burning. I could look down and see this–this kind of Dante's Inferno, this fire burning, and these people living under cardboard boxes, where they sleep, right on the garbage. And I looked across and I could see the places we were staying in San Diego. I could see streetlights, paved streets, hotel lights on, that kind of imagery on the other side of the border. Just looking back and forth and all of a sudden seeing that aircraft carrier come in–it was a moment that was very startling for me.

The second quarter I was at GTU, Dan Berrigan showed up to teach a course on nonviolence and one on the Book of Revelations. I took his courses and spent some time with him and got to know him a little bit, and he arranged for Daniel Ellsberg to come over to our house and I got to know him, too. The kinds of things they were saying were so startling, so interesting, so beautiful, I had to pursue them. And so using these two people as my tutors, I decided that something really needed to be done. And my life has been forever changed by that.

I finished a master's in theology at Berkeley, all the while getting more intense in my desire to be thoroughly disobedient to the laws this country has to protect nuclear weapons and trying to think of ways I can arrange my life so I can be away from my family, my family can be supported, we can live in prayer, that kind of thing.

One of the experiments we continue to struggle with is trying to live in community. Because we've discovered that if we all share a little bit more we'll have a lot more time to attend to some of the global needs, even just neighborhood needs of people who live around us who are in a bad way. So we've been struggling with community. Sometimes under the same roof and sometimes as intentional neighbors. But people who were deliberately putting themselves together to be a resistance community and a prayer community. We shared household chores and developed campaigns against weapons facilities in the Oakland area.

I think the prayer we need to speak of these days is the prayer of our lives. It means we start caring about each other in concrete, day-to-day ways, and that we take moments of quiet to be together and pray more traditionally on a regular basis. I think the greatest mistake happening in the church is that prayer has gotten relegated to the altar and to a church building. Our prayer needs to be taken into the streets. If we're going to pray about life, maybe the best place to do that is next to nuclear bunkers, at soup kitchens, in hospitals, jails, those kinds of places where the forces of death are so obvious. That's where life can be proclaimed.

I think there's been incredible damage done to the collective human soul by the last forty years of nuclear terror. You begin to see that people have been seduced into thinking the MX can be a peacekeeper. That somehow these things are life-giving, that they protect us, when the truth of the matter is whether or not the bomb ever goes off, for many, it's already gone off.

We've already become destroyed by neglecting the thirty or forty thousand children under five years old that will die today of starvation. Today. For most of the world, the bomb going off is irrelevant to their daily life. That is the situation for most of the world. Most of the world is faced with death and torture and extermination and deliberate neglect. The fact of life for the Third World is they are dying from the effects of the bomb.

It seems pretty clear there is a massive lie abroad that partly has to do with the idea that it's impossible for us to deal with megadeath. We can deal with megatons and kilotons much easier than we can deal with megadeath. There's a denial that goes so deeply into our own souls that we can actually come out believing those terrible, terrible instruments of destruction and the whole military whirlwind going on in the world, that that is actually in service of life.

It keeps us denying the present holocaust, it denies the future possibilities if these bombs go off. It freezes us into going about our business because somehow we can't do anything about it because it paralyzes us. It paralyzes good people. We no longer see the options. For me, I'm looking to take responsibility, whatever little part, whatever minute part I can lend to this massive problem. I need to be one person who says, "As for me, if you will continue, you will do it over my body. You will not do it with my approval."

It seems to me that the way to reclaim our humanity, to be alive, to recapture our passion for living and embrace those children is to begin to say no to what's going on. Categorically, I will not pay my taxes. I will go

over the fence to the army depot as we did on December 28. I will live in
community. I will live poorly. I will live and breathe with the people that
are suffering because of this, and I will find a way to raise my voice, to say
no.

From the time we're kids these days, we are saturated with a culture
that would have us believe and do the most outrageous things. People don't
even know how to be in a relationship any more. Many marriages are
ending in divorce; many kids are from broken homes of some sort or
another. Unemployment is up, kids are being beaten, wives are being
beaten. There's tremendous stress. People are killing themselves because
they're losing their jobs. The society is at a personal breaking point. And
those kinds of people who are living in that world of family disintegration
are then the people who have to make – who get elected, who end up
making decisions about whether to use a bomb. If our leaders are growing
up in a personally destructive environment, we've had it.

If I can't make a decision about how to keep a personal relationship, if I
can't even be in a one-to-one relationship with you, how in the world am I
going to make a decision about the relationship of my country to another?
If I can't care about you, if I can't care about the people who are right next
door – there is a brothel on this street, there are welfare people, people
being evicted – if I can't do that, I'll never expect myself to be able to make
decisions about global relationships. I can only act globally out of a context I've learned personally.

The problem is so much one of relationships, of trying to understand that
out of our enemies – the Russians, the Chinese, somebody – out of those
enemies we can try to make friends. That out of the friends we have in our
own lives, we try to make better friends, try to keep them, try to nurture
them. I'm very sustained on a human level by friends who are also doing
good things and inspire me. I'm always very glad when I hear and jealous
that I'm not with them, when I hear of an action that people have been
jailed. I think there are a few people around who are keeping hope alive.

Andy Hirsch

Born and raised in Cleveland, Andy now lives in the suburb of Parma Heights, with his wife and six children. From a typical Catholic upbringing, he and his "little family group" have undergone a transformation as radical perhaps as the change that has swept the monolithic Latin American church into base communities.

9

I like to describe our little family group as parallel with the church rather than in opposition. The church is just very huge. The parish that we all belong to has over six thousand families. It's so big, so hard to do anything. We just had a need to be able to come together and share our faith and pray together, and to do things as families. We've been doing this for six or seven years. Only in the last three years have we done them together as families, just to do what we felt was important.

It's unfortunate because the Catholic Church has tremendous power for change. My sense is the bishops are so far ahead of the parishes that the bishops can write what they may, and I don't know how you make it work unless the pastors really believe it. The problem I see is that if you're a pastor of a large suburban parish, or any parish, your first agenda is keeping the buildings whole. I feel pastors think their mission is to keep that parish visible, and visible means in terms of buildings, not necessarily visible in terms of the love people have for each other, the quality of spiritual life. I think it's hard to preach social gospel when you're counting on people to send in their pledges. It becomes obvious to me as I'm getting older that the message of poverty in the Gospel is really paramount in order to do something. Because as long as you're tied to those buildings and those structures, as long as you have to pay utilities and janitors, you're always going to have to ask for money. And when you ask for money, you sometimes have to compromise. The question is, this is where we are as a church today. We've got these billions of dollars in buildings. What do we do with them?

We're only five families. We were six. One of our couples got divorced, and we haven't worked through that whole issue of what we do. We have strong feelings for both the woman and the man; we've got to face that issue. What is the Christian response? To just accept people. We don't understand divorce, but it happens. But we haven't dealt with it.

At some point you have to say, "We have to use our own gifts and talents and do the things that we can do." Next Sunday we're doing, "I found a gem and I want to share it with you." All we ask people to do is in their reading over the next two weeks, if something really jumps out at you – and you say, "Wow, I didn't know that," or, "I'm really moved by that" – to bring that to the group in a sentence or a paragraph. And then tell the group why that was important to you or why that stands out. And then have the group respond to it. It can come from any source, religious or secular.

We get together each Epiphany to celebrate those days. We try to pick some of the holy days. We try to make them meaningful to the families. These are family days. So we meet as families. We celebrate a seder meal, we celebrate Good Friday, we celebrate the beginning of Advent. We celebrate spring by going out to the park; we do it in the fall to say good-bye to summer. These are family events where all the kids are together with the adults. Then twice during the month just the adults get together, the ten of us, and we're geared towards adult discussions.

Small groups and the concept of building these roots – these are strong roots as the basis of the peace movement growing, in a way that can become a true moral force in the world. I think there's something about building from the bottom up that gives you that staying power to keep going, so it doesn't become faddish. The issue today is the freeze, and after the freeze we'll all go home and forget about it. The freeze is the first step, and I think the leaders, certainly in CALC, have pointed out this is step one towards a whole agenda of disarmament. Coming together in a small group and trying to come to grips with, What do I really believe? I read the Gospel, but do I believe it? Or are they just nice words that Jesus said? I follow the Commandments and pay my dues. But it's that internalizing of the Gospel spirit which says that people should be free, people have the right to exist. That love is the way, not guns and armament. I think that kind of message can only happen in the context of a dialogue in a group.

You can have charismatic preachers; everybody gets excited and they say yeah yeah yeah. I hear a lot of good speeches, and I read a lot of good literature, but I don't internalize it. I enjoy it for the moment and then I go on to other things. But when I have to sit and deal with it, when somebody challenges me, it becomes more a part of me. You begin to deal with the issues. If I believe this, then what am I going to do about it? How am I going to react to this new-found knowledge, this opening up of the spirit? It's the next steps that cause growth to occur.

I think a lot of people have conversion experiences. I've met so many. I've been saved; I've been born again. It's like after that happens, it's all over with. I'm saved is total. I have nothing else to do. I'm saying a true conversion experience is a process, and I think that process can only occur in a dialogue, a dialogue with yourself and a dialogue with others who are challenging you, who are bringing into question just what your beliefs are.

I think the next step after I have reached a conclusion or a belief is, What do I do about it? What actions show that this conversion experience has happened? For some, it's writing letters; for others, it's praying for peace; for others, it's walking in front of buildings with signs; for others, it's getting arrested at the shipyards or wherever they are. I think each person has to respond to that, and I don't think you all of a sudden decide that I'm going to go out and do civil disobedience without a long process of discernment. Is that really what I'm called to do? Doing that with the support of a community?

For me, six tuitions and a house mortgage, to go out and get arrested and three months in jail to me is not really listening to the spirit. But for a person who belongs to a community, and the community says if they arrest you, we'll take care of your house payment, we'll provide for your children, because we support what you are doing. We don't feel called to that kind of action, but we support you in that action. That's where I think peace communities have freed people to make those responses. The people in Seattle, those in Washington, DC, those who are going to the boatyards on the East Coast, have support back home. It's hard to be all alone and do these things.

I was reading in *Sojourners* about the Humanistic Psychology Association sponsoring a picture exchange with people in Russia. I thought, Wow, that would be great for the kids, because I'm sure when you say Russian, the children immediately think of the enemy.

It seems part of the thing we have to do is help people believe that the Russians are human and have the same needs we have for a nice home, food on the table, a job, for some of the extras, a car or whatever it is. And their goal in life is not to conquer the world. One of the ways we thought we could do it was to exchange pictures and hopefully eventually letters, just to share our humanness as families. It seemed to be a way that we could connect the kids with the issue. My children don't get excited about problems of defense spending, and I guess when I was twenty-one I wasn't concerned about it either. What we're hoping to do is to show the kids that home can be church. And it's something you just do experientially.

We wrote our addresses on the pictures, each individual address. Each family will be getting a response from a Russian family. After we get those responses, at another one of our family days, we will incorporate that experience and try to deal with it in terms of – tell us something about your Russian family. Who are they? What did they do?

Aggie Hoskins, who is part of our community and who works for the Isaiah Center, was constantly urging us to deal with issues. Last year she got me to picket for the first time. In forty-six years of my life, I never car-

ried a sign, participated in a demonstration. All during Lent we demon-
strated in front of the Federal Building against the Trident submarine.
That was my first experience. It just seemed like that was the right thing
to do. That led me to believe people have to begin to do something to
awaken the consciousness of America. We're sleeping.

I think back to the days of the sixties when all the hippies were demon-
strating against the Vietnam War and I was on the side of the government. I just didn't understand those people. They're un-American; we're
fighting the communists. I always thought of America as always right;
we're on the side of good, and we would never do anything that was not for
the good of the world. And it was only in the later literature that you discovered, for lack of better words, it was just screwed up from the beginning, and nobody had the balls to stand up and say we made a mistake.
From one administration to the other we perpetuated the error, and it was
only Nixon, under tremendous pressure, both people and budget, who
finally said we're getting out.

I'm really concerned about the tremendous dollars we spend in the military. I can't believe that people in power don't see the poverty and the
people that don't have food, don't have shelter, don't have jobs. It's like
saying, "I'm going to make sure that you can die in peace; boy, those Communists will never get you. You can die, but we'll protect you so you can die
on this American soil." And I just can't fathom it. I've written my congressmen; they just do not respond. How can you do this? The military has
a grocery list of things that is unending, and they get practically everything they want. I'm saying, Gee, in my own family, I have a fixed income
and to prioritize, we can do this, this and this. Or we can just do this. We
can't do everything because we don't have the money. The government
merely prints more money. It just blows my mind.

Why do we send guns and not wheat? Why do we support dictatorships?
Why is the human rights issue no longer an issue in this administration?
And why is it all right to imprison, to kill, to hold people without trial, and
yet we still support these governments because we say they're somehow
democratic? I would be apprehensive about traveling to Latin America,
because I don't know how I would be received as a North American. I feel
we're doing terrible things down there in the name of good government or
trying to protect people in power against so-called communists. This idea
of communists and evil being one – I just don't believe that.

I have written Reagan and said, "You've got to talk to people. You can't
say we aren't going to move till they do this or they do that. Someplace
you've got to start talking. I don't see how the office of the president would
be discredited because you met with Soviet leaders and said, Guys, your

economy's hurting, our economy's hurting, you got enough to blow us up, we got enough to blow you up. If we want to stay in power we better start doing something for our people. That just makes so much sense to me. Reagan has said he can only deal from a position of strength. That doesn't say too much to me because if you're holding a gun on me and saying I want you to speak to me, I don't have a whole lot of options, so I don't know if we ever really come together as long as you're holding that gun.

My hope is by doing simple things, like exchanging pictures, somehow that this will stay with my children, and they'll say, "Hey, that's important, and we want to do that, too." I think the government's only going to turn around when the great majority of the people want the government to turn around. As long as it's just a small group, they will always be known as the pinkos or the radicals or however you want to label them. It's the middle class the government listens to. The poor are always screaming. So if we can get the middle class people to write their congressmen to say, "I want peace; I want the military budget reduced; I want grain to go overseas; I want you to go talk to our adversaries; I want you to get out of these countries in Latin America and let them find their own destiny" – I think they will begin to listen. I'm hopeful. It's not going to happen as quickly as I want it; I'm just hopeful that reason will prevail and we won't do something radical.

Carrie Dickerson

Almost single-handedly, Carrie Dickerson, a nurse in the small town of Claremore, Oklahoma, stopped the nearby construction of Black Fox nuclear power plant. She prevailed against all odds, largely because of her incredible determination and perseverance. While the nine-year-long legal battle has taken its toll financially and physically, one can only hope that her courage, and rest, will restore her from exhaustion.

10

I had never seen a child with leukemia until I took nurses' training in the late sixties. I went back at the age of fifty because we had a nursing home, needed an RN, and couldn't find one. I went back and became one. And this little child, about five years old, beautiful brown-eyed little boy, was not able to walk. He had to be carried. His mother was there with him. He was in and out of the hospital, just lethargic. A little five-year-old is really bouncy and full of energy. He was not the normal little five-year-old, but he was a precious little boy.

My daughter – she was a student with me – took care of him the second semester. We had him together, the full care of him when he was in the hospital, the whole nine months. We saw him progessively get worse. Then, I didn't know about nuclear power, but it certainly gave me an insight into what the ravages of leukemia can be to a child.

I had been out of nurses' training three years when on May 8, 1973, someone laid a paper on my desk. I came in and saw the big headlines, $450 Million N-Plant Planned for Inola, and I thought, what in the world is an N-Plant? They hadn't named it Black Fox yet. My curiosity got the better of me, and I thought, What's an N-Plant? Then I thought, Oh, a nuclear plant, sure enough, nuclear. I read on. It was a four-page article touting the benefits of nuclear power – too cheap to meter and all this stuff. Safest means of producing electricity there is. And I thought, Well, I wonder. And somehow a picture came back to my mind that I had seen at least twenty years, about twenty years earlier when I taught school in Claremore.

I was teaching home ec, and I was in the library. *Life* magazine was open on a table. As I passed by, this little picture of a muskrat caught my eye. I stopped and read the caption which stated, "This muskrat was caught, and this muskrat has cancer." The muskrat was caught in the tributaries below Oak Ridge nuclear facility in Oak Ridge, Tennessee, and it was determined the cancer was caused by the radioactive effluent from the nuclear facility at Oak Ridge. That had stayed in my mind, and at the time I thought, Oh, how dreadful.

I was a pretty naive person twenty years earlier, thirty years ago now. I was thirty-six. I thought, Surely our government will take care of that. I won't have to worry about it. I dismissed it from my mind. But when I read that article, I thought, Has the government taken care of it? It's strange that that lay dormant in my mind, and all of a sudden I could see that picture and remembered that caption. I thought, I'll find out.

I called Washington and asked the Atomic Energy Commission to send me everything a common citizen could understand about nuclear power. They sent me reams of material. It was their information that sold me against nuclear power because they had just released, a few months before I called, a study that had been commissioned in 1964. The scientists were to determine what would happen if the water were cut off from a nuclear power plant. And they found in their study that there would be a meltdown. That's where the China Syndrome thing came from.

This study that I read had just been released because Ralph Nader, through the Freedom of Information Act, required that it be made public. And so it was. And when they sent it to me, I read it, and it said that an area the size of Pennsylvania would be destroyed for habitation. That's prophetic, you know. This was in 1973.

After reading for three months, I told my husband I had to start fighting, or talking to people. Other people need to know this. Because I was getting armloads of material, and I knew that not more than maybe a half-dozen people in Oklahoma were even knowledgeable of nuclear power. At least I hadn't found any. He said, "You can't get involved in a fight on nuclear power. Your life could be in jeopardy." That was his exact statement. And I said, "But Robert, what's my life compared to our little grandson, who's not even two? If I'm afraid for my life and sit and hold my hands, then I couldn't live with myself if he got leukemia, or any other child. My life wouldn't be worth living." I didn't need nurses' training to know what cancer was.

My husband also objected to me going into the fight against nuclear power because he realized it was tied together with nuclear arms, like Siamese twins. Uranium is necessary for nuclear bombs and nuclear power, he said. And the corporations and the people who own stock and who own these companies are in it for the money – they're not farsighted enough to see that they themselves could be destroyed too, by either. They're interested in just a short-term gain.

But anyway, I began asking organizations, churches or what have you, to let me talk. Most people just turned me off. The public service company was asking every city council, or whatever the governing body, to give their approval of Black Fox. Everyone in a twenty-five-mile radius. The city council here was to vote on it the first week of September. This was in the paper, and a lady from Inola called me, a friend, and said I must go to that council meeting. I took a packet, a duplication of everything that was very pertinent, and gave a thiry-minute talk. The next day, there was a big article in the paper at the very top of the front page quoting my statements. With every statement, there was a rebuttal by the PR person from the public service company. It made me look like a fool.

It's the best thing that could have happened because it gave publicity. I got calls from all over the state, and one call, the first call, they asked the name of our organization. And I thought, Boy, if you admit you don't have an organization, you're lost. I had seen Ralph Nader a few days earlier on TV talking about nuclear power, and his citizen action groups. I just thought, Well, Ralph won't mind. So I called it Citizens' Action Group.

My mother always told me, don't ever tell the first lie. You have to back it up with the second lie. The second question was: And how many people in your organization? I thought, God, provide one hundred people, so I said, "Oh, about one hundred." It was real interesting, though. This came out in the paper, and I started getting phone calls. People wanted to be my 101st member. And before I knew it, I had 101 members. We had a ready-made organization that we changed later to Citizens' Action for Safe Energy.

This is a very conservative state, a very fundamentalist state. This is what's called the Bible Belt. People here take things literally. You're not supposed to go against the status quo.

In the very beginning, three church women came to see me after the first article came out in the *Claremore Progress*, and they sat down in my office and said, "Carrie, as a Christian, you are not doing the right thing. You know that you're going against the precepts of the Bible." And I said, "How in the world am I doing that?" And they said, "First, you're not supposed to fight the government." I said, "I'm not fighting the government; I am one part of this government. Of the people, by the people, for the people. And if I don't do my duty as one part of this government, then we will become like Hitler's Germany." Then they really took me to task. They said, "Well, this is the way God is going to destroy the world, the earth. And we have to accept it." Just like our own Interior Secretary, Mr. Watt. Is this a legend or is it the truth that he said Christ was coming within three or four years, so we need to use it up? I've read that he said it.

People called me a communist. They wrote letters to the editor. I decided in the very beginning that in order to survive I had to develop a real thick skin, and that was difficult. I became very ill after reading and studying and after these first reactions of people. I started having nightmares. My scalp broke out in sores, huge sores, because of tension and stress. I had to say, "God, you're going to have to take over these burdens. You're going to have to give me a free mind and help me. I can't cope if I'm ill, and I have to." As if I were my own psychiatrist, I had to say, "You have to ignore some of this, and some of it you have to just come back to later. For right now, Carrie, just have tunnel vision."

Our first attorney was one of the most brilliant men I've ever known. He was so smart; he dug and researched – it was amazing the things he came up with. Because the AEC law was not in our favor, he had every kind of delaying tactic you can imagine. But when he'd meet with us he'd say, "There is no hope of stopping the plant, the only thing you can do is improve the safety measures." Well, I was sitting there saying to myself, "God, you know we can stop that plant, just in the meantime, don't listen to him!" Meanwhile I would tell the attorney, "We *are* going to stop this plant, and don't you leave one stone unturned!"

As a result of the first set of hearings the company was awarded a limited work authorization, and we had to get a second set of attorneys. We had so many appeals going. I had to send them to Washington to learn the AEC law. I had to send them to San Jose, California, to study with our expert witnesses, the MHB Technical Associates. It was a big endeavor, and as I couldn't raise the money I took it out of our pocket – we had sold the nursing home the year before.

When all the attorneys called a meeting and recommended we pull out, just quit, I said, "No, I'll never quit." And they said, "This is going to be more costly than you can bear." And I said, "Don't you worry about the cost. I'll worry about the cost. You worry about doing the job and doing it right. I have forty acres that belong to me alone. My uncle left my twin sister and me eighty acres. I'll sell my forty and get the money." They said, "You might as well quit now, you'll never win." I said, "No, we will win, and you don't have permission to quit. What will it take?" They said collateral. I said, "The only thing I have is the forty acres." They said that's all right. And they put a mortgage on that forty acres. What's forty acres compared to lives?

Finally, all the hearings were completed, March 1979. Less than a month later, Three Mile Island happened. I have no doubt that had Three Mile Island not happened, the public service company would have been issued a construction permit. The attorneys told me that, too. Three Mile Island caused a freeze on construction permits everywhere. The attorneys said, "We're so thankful you persevered, because if you'd allowed us to quit, if those hearings hadn't been delayed, Black Fox would have been built."

There's one thing that I had to learn in this. About the sores that broke
out on my head because I was angry – I had to overcome this. I was so
angry at the public service company and the government I had to ask God
to just keep me from being angry. And in order to keep from being angry,
you have to learn to love. I had to treat those people as if they were my
family; I had to love them. And you know, they started treating me the
same. I found out they were human beings just like I am. And they were
really great people. I've never understood how they could reason like they
did, but still, they'd come to the hearings, and they'd come and sit down
beside me and put their arm around me. They were just as nice as they
could be, like I was their old grandmother to them or something.

Bill and Darrell Breedon

Bill and Darrell Breedon, twin brothers, live together with their families on a remote farm in rural southwestern Indiana, Daviess County. Opting out of the middle class, each family lived on $1,200 last year, perhaps even less this year. They are home-schoolers and gifted, authentic indigenous musicians. Outside of Daviess County, they have performed their music in Washington, and at Riverside Church in New York City.

11

Bill: This is a conservative area, but our group, the Daviess County Peace and Justice Coalition, began collecting proxies for the freeze, and we were astounded by the fact that 80 percent of the doors that we knocked on signed the proxies. And the ones that didn't sign, we really had very few hostile reactions. Most of those that didn't sign just didn't understand what it was.

We kept getting the answer, There's nothing you can do; and yet the end result was many of them said, "This is fine that there's something I *can* do." I told them I'm going to deliver this personally to our senators and our congressmen, which I did. I think Senator Quayle was really impressed, not that he's going to change his mind. I think we gave Quayle over eighty thousand proxies for the freeze. We told him, 80-some percent of the doors that we knocked on signed it. It surprised him. And it showed people in western Indiana that at least there was something they could do to voice their opinion.

Darrell: I for one think it's going to take more than citizens lobbying the Congress to change the arms race. I just don't think it's going to happen that easily. The war wasn't stopped by lobbying, it was stopped by people in the streets saying this is it. We're not going to take any more. I think we're going to see some exciting times in the eighties, very exciting times.

Bill: I went to Nashville Theology School, to college, basically to be a preacher. The problem we have in our society is ignorance, and I don't mean that in a derogatory way. I think ignorance is just a lack of knowledge. The problem is that our schools are not educating to the truth. We get a warped sense of history; we get hero worship rather than history. So I went to college, a very racist and narrow-minded person who thought Davis County represented most of the world. I found out different, rather quickly. I met black people in ghettos who were human, very hungry people, and I couldn't reconcile the hatred of blacks with the Gospel that I was supposedly being trained to preach.

About 1979 I was associate pastor in a large church in Missouri and was hitchhiking to Louisville to hear Dan Berrigan and some other people from Mobilization for Survival. I was somewhat of a radical by that time, but not in any way, shape or form ready to go out and hit the streets. Well, through providence or fate or bad luck or whatever, I got let out about one o'clock in the morning on December 7, 1979. The windchill factor was below zero, and I ended up walking nineteen miles in a state of despair, freezing and everything else. At one point at the Church Rock turnoff on I-70, I realized that I was only four hundred yards from a one megaton missile. The Minuteman system, that "Nuclear Valley of Death" we have out there. I stood there and wept. That's probably the most radically life-changing event I've ever experienced.

I got back that weekend, and Brenda and I realized that things were never going to be the same again. We had to get out there and stop it. We owned a house; we were very middle class, very successful in the ministry and all this, but it didn't mean anything if we were totally annihilated within thirty minutes. From that time on we decided that peace was the most important thing in the world. Those issues became more and more alive.

We resigned our church six months after that. I felt that I could no longer cooperate with the United States government. I feel it's not just the arms race – it's El Salvador, Nicaragua. I began to feel like a murderer by proxy. That my tax dollars were killing my brothers and sisters in Salvador and all over. I can't help the Soviet system; I can't change that. If I were in Soviet Russia I'd probably be in prison, or a psychiatric ward. But my tax dollars are not paid to the Kremlin. They're paid to Washington; they pay for the Pentagon.

We decided to drop out of the middle class, and we decided that as long as there are poor in our country, we would be poor by choice. Last year we had a total income of about $1,200, my wife and two children and I. And we had a roof over our heads, and we had food on the table. And this year we probably haven't kept up with that. But we have two families together now, so we live much cheaper. We have a situation here where this elderly woman owns this farm and wants the house kept up because it was falling down. So she charges us no rent as long as we improve it.

So we can live very cheap, and we feel like we're very lucky. I'm not necessarily proud about doing what we're doing, but we're very fortunate, because I have time with my family I've never had before. I know that all middle class people can't do that. I got a letter from a very close friend of mine not long ago saying that I'd at least opted out of the middle class guilt of wealth. I wrote him back saying I really am not interested in weighing it on a scale of righteousness. I've got my own guilt, and I live with that. It's just the choices we made. We feel like we want to teach our children that they do not have to be dependent on an economic system in order to survive. Give them some alternatives.

Darrell: Bill and I, our families were separated for ten years. We're twins. Bill went to Missouri to the seminary. I went to Missouri for a year and moved back to Terre Haute, Indiana. I was working in a factory. My change came about a lot because of all the values I'd been taught. Personal conversion, personal salvation type thing we were raised in. Bill and I in fact were revivalists since we were about fifteen. We traveled revival meetings and this sort of thing, saving souls for Jesus. Suddenly at about twenty-five years old it just all didn't mean anything to me. It just kind of fell out from under me.

My marriage was on the verge of collapse. I was on the verge of collapse. It came to a point of almost self-destruction. I started looking at myself and wondering how I got here. I'd never drank anything hardly in my life or used drugs or anything else, and suddenly for about a year that's all I did do—just totally self-destructive things. I kept asking myself, How did I get here? All this I've been taught in world history, this couldn't happen to me. It's not supposed to happen to people like me, and it did. I was at the point of just giving up on everything.

Bill came home from Missouri to talk to me, spend a week with me. We started talking, and I realized we had gone through a lot of the same things, only he'd found different answers. I think that's partly because of his education; his study of the scriptures led to a lot different answers than we'd been given. Somehow or other we started to think about putting things back together and find a real sense of purpose for my life, which was getting involved in the peace movement. All the time we'd been going around saving people for Jesus in our revivals and everything else, we hadn't changed anything. We were just kind of pie-in-the-sky religion, selling people a peace of heaven.

Christians prosper type of thing. If you're poor it's because God's not favoring you. And God Bless America. I heard a sermon just a year ago on Memorial Day about how God's blessed our nation and enriched it right here in Odom, Indiana, and how we're so blessed because God loves us. I wanted to ask the guy, Why don't you come to Chicago with me and I'll show you some people maybe God doesn't love so much. Middle class America, and especially rural America, doesn't see that.

We heard an evangelist one time on the radio talking about seven or fifteen-ninety-five or so many dollars—it was back during the Biafran thing—that you could send a cassette and take the Gospel to everybody in Biafra. People were dropping dead starving to death, and he was going to send cassette tapes of the Gospel. It's just that kind of insanity. I started seeing a whole new thing in the Gospel of peace, and it gave my life new direction and purpose that it never had before. That's where we come to now.

In every church in southern Indiana you're going to find an American flag. When they try to say the church doesn't have any business in the peace movement because of separation of church and state, I say the church taught me nation worship. The state has always been in the church in my experience. Honor God and country. I couldn't swear; we didn't swear or go to movies; as Bill used to say, we didn't smoke, drink or chew, or go with girls that do. That was our Christian – to be Christian, and yet I could kill, and I could hate. Hate wasn't a four-letter word; I could hate niggers. Nigger wasn't a four-letter word, that's all right. I learned all this in the church.

Bill: I never read the Bible when I was a kid. I was told to read the Bible, but what that meant was pick out a scripture before you go to bed kind of thing, at random. Or if you had a problem, you took the Bible and threw it on the bed, and wherever it opened up there was an answer there somewhere. Kind of superstition. But nobody ever told me to sit down and read that Bible and find out what's there. When you do, you find a tremendous emphasis on peace and justice. Sure there's war there; sure there's stories about God killing people and everything else because the Bible grows up. And their concept of God grows with them as this book develops.

One of the most radical things that ever happened to me was to have an assignment in seminary to rewrite the minor prophets in my own words. You get with the minor prophets, you're getting with guys, you're dealing with the Berrigans of their day. Those minor prophets were crazy, nuts. They stood radically opposed to the system. They were hated by the church; they were hated by the nation because they cried out for the poor. I think that that identification with the minor prophets probably is the most important identification that I have.

My definition of a religious person is one who's concerned about life and preserving life, and continuing this beautiful human race. I think those are the kind of people that are going to have to fill up the jails in this country in order to bring about a change. And I think they probably will.

Darrell: I grew up – I was very poorly educated. I made good grades in school, and yet as far as history, I knew nothing. I talk to high school students – we get to talking about history. "I hate history," they say. And the reason they hate history is because it's not true. You take the teaching of history in Indiana. A recent survey we read said that in the history books of high schools in Indiana, the largest segment concerning the bombing at Hiroshima was one paragraph. That's the largest segment in any of the history books in Indiana. As far as our lifetimes, it was the most significant event ever. Not only our lifetimes, but this entire century. The most life-changing thing that's happened. It's utterly ignored. The causes and the aftermath of it. The Vietnam War, another case in point. They don't teach *The Pentagon Papers* in public schools. Look at what they teach about the Vietnam War – it's still glorified. We have a president who calls it a noble cause ten years after the fact. It's insanity. I don't think the public schools are so much a tool of education as they are a tool of control.

Bill: When we were in Kentucky, we were forced to put the kids back into school. I got thrown in jail, and then I got out of that for a while. We got an ex-military court martial judge. He wouldn't let me say a word in court. In a second hearing I began singing because he wouldn't let me talk. Glenda and the children left the state for a while, and then they came back, and we just stayed incommunicado with the county for a while. We had our own school for three and a half months without them bothering us. Then one day they showed up in a sheriff's car and took the kids away from us and put them in foster homes. They never asked a question about education, not one single thing. We compromised; we wanted to keep that from happening, of course, because I couldn't see our kids get taken from us. But they took legal custody of our children without any hearings, nothing. They just came and got 'em. And the teachers, the very first day of class, met with the social worker and said these kids are ahead of the class. They're being taught; somebody's teaching them. They're well ahead of the class. The principal told our neighbors, "We can't teach those kids; their parents ought to be teaching them." But the judge wouldn't let us. Freedom is a good concept, but try to live it.

I watched the school. I went to the school, and they wouldn't let us have a school in our home because – we had a 120-acre farm that we were caretaking – because we didn't have a legal playground with a hundred square yards of asphalt, a technicality. I've never seen such chaos on the playground than in the public school. The way it's controlled is the thing that came home to me as I sat by the playground and watched.

I wrote a poem about this, because I sat there and watched for six hours that day, just observing the public school system. The title is "Line Up, Kids, When the Whistle Blows." It goes like this:

> Line up, kids, when the whistle blows
> It makes marching fun so no one knows
> Someday you'll join the endless ranks
> Of those who march with guns and tanks.
>
> It's necessary to go to school
> So you can learn the golden rule.
> Not the one of love that everyone knows,
> But the rule to line up when the whistle blows.

Learn well now of law and order
So when the time comes to cross the border
To kill and maim this nation's foes,
You'll all line up when the whistle blows.

I think that's basically what we have in public education. The children are taught to keep law and order, but they're not taught love, they're not taught the things that make for peaceful coexistence. We have classes in football and beating each other, hitting each other, all kinds of violence. We *don't* have classes on peacemaking.

Harry Truman said in 1948 that the only country in the world that has a better propaganda system than the Soviet Union, than Uncle Joe Stalin's Russia, was the United States of America. He was talking about public education. We don't need state control here by force because we are much more subtle and able to do it without that. Television – look at television – look at what comes across on the news. We don't need it. We got rid of ours and never felt freer. You can see why people aren't involved. You can see why people think we're communists or radicals, because Ronald Reagan gets up right on national television and says the peace movement is being run by the KGB. And where does he get his source but the *Reader's Digest*? And then the *Reader's Digest* quotes him. Neither one of them gives you any information. But thirty million people read the *Reader's Digest*, and eighty million watch Reagan.

There's a Greek word the Biblical writers used continually – *chiros*, as opposed to *chronos*, which simply means "time". *Chiros* means "pregnant time," a time that's about to burst open and give birth to something new. And I think we're in a *chiros* time. About a year ago I came to a point between cynicism and hope. If you sit down rationally to figure things out, it's very easy to take the road of cynicism and say, This isn't going to change, it's impossible, we're small, they're too big. But when I look into the eyes of my children, I can't do that. I have to say, By God, there is hope. Because there are children out there. And there are a lot of adults out there who are still crazy enough to be children. And whenever you've got children around, systems don't work very well. You can't regiment them too much because they're going to break loose and do something free.

Mattie Jones

Long a force, not just in the black community but in all of Louisville, Mattie Jones was the recipient of the 1983 Peace and Justice Award of the Catholic Peace and Justice Council. Perhaps her life is an embodiment of Paul's admonition, "Be angry, but do not sin."

12

I've been aware of injustice for a very very long time. I came out of Central High School in the year 1951. I went to an all-black school. There were no equal schools at that time. There were black schools, white schools, and we got the books that the white folks did not need. We even had a Catholic school on 8th Street, called Catholic Colored High. All around me everything was letting me know that I was a black person, a black young woman hoping to become a woman in this society. There were colored fountains, white fountains. All of this . . . And what really really just made me *damn* mad was when I was a student out at the University of Louisville. I needed a PE course, so I said I'll take bowling. So I signed up for bowling. When I went to the gym that day the instructor told me that I could not take bowling. I said, "Why not?" And he said, "Well, where would you bowl?" That made me damn mad. I said something's got to be done with this.

I went to the dean and raised holy hell. I asked him how did he differentiate between my mother's money and the elite lady's money. How do you do this? You got separate cash registers? How do you do this kind of thing? I went round and round, and finally I got the choice of taking fencing, and I was very appreciative. My instructor was the only one that would be my partner.

Then along came the fight for open housing and public accommodation here in Louisville in the fifties and the early sixties. I joined in helping brothers and sisters all over the city fight to tear the barriers down. I made up my mind that somebody had to help fight and help tear down this kind of racism. It just could not exist. I was *damn* mad.

This is what has kept me going. Because I don't believe in just sitting here at home, knowing these things exist. You do something. If you don't do something when you know anything, then this power monster will take over everything. He'll take your own soul if that's what it takes for him to get ahead. So as a woman, especially as a black woman that has known racism all her life, you get out here and you do something. I don't want my grandchildren and great grandchildren to have to fight a battle as hard as I have fought just to survive.

I'm chairperson of the Kentucky Alliance to End Racism and Political Oppression. I have always had the consciousness of community needs on my mind. I fought for a long time as a soloist, but then I began to realize you can't just fight this battle all by yourself, you've got to join with some organization. I worked with the Black Workers Coalition awhile and then I attended several meetings of the alliance. I enjoyed their work and I liked their perspective, so I finally became a member. Since that time we have addressed a lot of things that affect the black community. We've dealt very hard with police brutality.

We've always been the last to be hired. We've been the first to be fired. We've never even had equal salary to the whites. We had to fight for certain areas of cities, sections to live. We've had to fight for education for our children. This is a part that we've always known. Everything we've ever gained, we had to demand.

This country's going to get a hell of a damn surprise. During the Vietnam era, that middle class white boy that didn't want to fight and realized that it was wrong, he was able to skip on over to Canada. During that time, young blacks were not familiar with the wrongness of Vietnam. So the ones they recruited into the service were the poor man's children, and black children. Now the tables have turned. Our boys have been there. They know how vicious America is. Because after they went to Vietnam, when they came home, the treatment they got after fighting this country's cruel war was more racism.

The young men, and young women, that they recruited had no other economic means of survival. That's one reason they got so many. They were caught between the depths and the deep blue sea. Now they are not going to get young folks to fight their dirty battles. They're going to have to get the hell out of El Salvador, Central America. And what they're trying to do now – and the kids see this – they're trying to put this country into total hysteria about how many nuclear weapons Russia has and why we need so many MX missiles and all of these things.

People starving to death and freezing to death in the land of the free. Right here in this country. People in this country eating out of garbage cans, living under subways, in cardboard boxes, any kind of way they can live. And they still want to take all of the money and put it into nuclear arms.

Every damn body up there in Washington is mad; every damn body up there is crazy. After they get all these things built, they haven't looked at the minds of the people. They're not going to get folks in this country to say yes, increase this military budget. They're getting the message every day. The people do not want it. The people are saying, You don't take away bread from hungry folks to build military arms, to do the same kind of mess you're trying to do over in El Salvador what you did in Vietnam.

It's the top leadership that wants these things. It's not the people. That's why if this government, this type of madness doesn't stop, it's not communism that's going to overthrow your damn government, hell, it's the people who're going to overthrow it. They're not going to be hungry; they're not going to be living outdoors while you build all of these weapons to fight a war which does not have any kind of meaning. You can't explain or give any kind of meaning about why you need all of these things. That's why they keep trying to whip up this war hysteria. This is why they're telling eighteen-year-olds you must register for the draft or you will be arrested.

My fear is that all of this is going to lead to a war like the war between the north and south, like the Civil War. Only it's not going to be the north against south, it's going to be people versus the power structure.

People are taking over. Look what happened in Rhodesia. Rhodesia claimed their freedom and they became Zimbabwe. And I do believe that very very soon, and I don't mean next year, South Africa is going to win her freedom. And poor people, minority folk in this country, we're going to win our freedom against this monster. I see it coming. You can call it a revolution. They can call it a war or whatever you want to call it, but it's got to happen. Somebody's got to stop them, and nothing's going to stop them but people. People are beginning – and thank God for the young folks that had the courage to go over the fences of the nuclear plants – people more and more are seeing this as a war between themselves and the power structure. And they are saying, No, we're not going to take it. We don't care what happens to us because there's going to be more that will come. And then we'll be back again to the days where we have good brothers and sisters.

A lot of times, this violent way is the only way that lets this country's superiors, government, know that folks are not going to take it, and they're tired of it. I know in my experience you can go to them, you can sit at the bargaining table, and they're so nice, they're so attentive. No one's going to do a damn thing. When you walk out the door, they slam it. But take a look at what happened in the sixties when the cities began to burn, then they got concerned. Folks are really fed up. This country was built on blood.

Take the Indians. They put them off on a reservation, said this is yours, gave them some land. They thought it was nothing and hoped to hell they would die. Now they've discovered that there's some richness in this soil they've given the Indians and they want to take it back. But the Indians are saying now wait a minute. And you look at them. At one time they only thought of themselves as certain tribes. I'm a Cherokee, or I'm a Choctaw or Sioux. Now they're coming together as Indians. They're moving into the peace movement; they're moving into the civil rights movement. They're becoming a part of the human rights issues.

When you talk about human rights and human needs, you're talking about living in this world as brothers and sisters. You're talking about not destroying things or taking away lives. You're talking about the right to freedom, for food, for shelter, for housing, education. You're talking about not having to fight your brother of color in the Third World countries. So the peace movement and civil rights movement go hand in hand to make this a human rights issue, of people living together in an atmosphere conducive to what the Lord says you're supposed to have.

I've raised eight children. Come May I'll see my eighth child graduate. They've all had high school, all been to college. I have some graduates and I have some with some hours. But the most important thing is they are living their own lives, they're self-sufficient. They're free.

I'm so glad that my children can say, I'm going bowling. I'm so happy that I carried them swimming at the Crescent Hill pool one afternoon. I said, Let me tell you about the struggle for you to be able to swim in that pool. We as black parents have not made our struggle known to them. They just don't realize that we had to do all of this for them to be able to go to an integrated school. They just don't know what it is that we had to live through for them to be able to sit anyplace on the bus, to go to the bowling alley, to be able to go swimming. During my time we had one little swimming pool, the 17th Street pool, and on Sunday afternoon there would be a thousand black children in a pool that would really only accommodate fifty. They don't know our history, and they don't know our struggle. And the white man is trying to remove it from them. This is the way that he thinks will be a way of keeping them down.

Our children come home in the afternoon and the only thing they can go to is the community center to play basketball. Hell, we all can't be basketball players. We may have talent beyond basketball. We might have some engineering talent, some tennis talent, but we don't cultivate it. We need to have a place for them to go to in the afternoon that is constructive instead of all these recreation, community centers that they build for us and we do nothing but play basketball. They don't even have reading rooms in these centers to tell you about black history. They don't even have a room where you can have a tutor if you're having some problems. All you do is play.

Believe it or not, in 1983 we had to go to the federal courts in order for Angela Davis to speak in the high school that once was a black high school, Central High, in the black community. The only reason that the school board told me that Angela could not speak at Central High School was because they would have to give equal time to the Klan. This is why I tell you the Klan has taken off their robes. Anybody with that kind of mentality doesn't have to belong to the Klan to carry out their practices.

A lot of folks say to me that Angela Davis is a communist. And I say to them, Angela wasn't always a communist. I don't know when she joined the Communist party, but I do know she was there in Birmingham when the church was bombed and the four little black girls died.

Stephen Mershon

Steve Mershon, a family lawyer and prosecutor, lives with his wife and young daughter in Louisville, Kentucky. He also teaches a course in "The Criminal Justice System and Spouse Abuse" for workers at the Jefferson County Spouse Abuse Center.

13

I went to a year of graduate school in psychology before law school. I was thinking about being a counselor. Then, going through law school, I thought, Well, I'll be a family lawyer, and I'll let people come to me and I'll work with them, and if I can't work with them and get their marriages back on track, then I'll just do the best to let them have a successful divorce. So at least if their marriage falls apart, I'll try to work for them so they can part ways on equitable and talking terms, and then let them both go on with their lives. And that's sort of the way my practice of law has just evolved. I've been very fortunate with my job as a county prosecutor because it's all been in the area of family law.

I started off doing child support and paternity actions. Now, I prosecute dependency, abuse and neglect cases, which was actually my first choice when I started practicing. The thing that I've learned in dealing with child abuse and spouse abuse both is that it's pretty much still a cycle. Which is just like world history. It's a cycle. We learn from our parents.

We find that very many of the men who abuse their spouses were themselves abused as children. And it's often not even something that a man wants to do, but out of fear and frustration and anger, and not knowing how else to deal with the problem, he'll strike out and just beat the tar out of his wife.

Nobody likes to break up marriages, but if you can't get the man to get some help to change his ways, it's better to break a marriage up and let the children grow up in a nonviolent atmosphere than it is just to keep the thing going. I really think that the international scene is just the domestic situation much bigger. It's the same way. We've been doing the same things for generations.

Things that seem most important to me are all in the area of prevention. It's the same way with war; it's the same way with spouse abuse, the same way with child abuse. If we spent money working on prevention, we might be able to stop the cycle before it gets started.

One of the things that most impresses me is this movement for a national peace academy. They're fighting in Congress now for appropriate monies for a national peace academy. They're asking for a minuscule amount of money, but they're trying to develop an academy to teach peace instead of war. We've got all the Navy, the Army, the Air Force; we've got all these different academies to teach people how to make war, but we don't have anything to teach people how to make peace. Internationally recognized principles of arbitration and negotiation and conciliation. If we can work towards those things we can teach people how to make peace.

At some point in time, somebody's gotta be brave enough to say, Well, they killed my brother; I'm not going to go back there and kill their brother. I'm going to go back with an olive branch and say, I lost my brother, I know how important your brother is to you. Let's start talking.

I was flashing back and thinking of football, because I played high school football for three years before I came to my senses and quit. We had an excellent coach, a man that I very much respected, but I can even remember one time getting in a fight on the football field, which was something – coaches got excited when you'd get in a fight, because that's what they wanted to see you do. They wanted to see you get angry and hit somebody. Football disturbs me, because I really think it's not a healthy sport. It's a very violent sport. And there's so many sports that can be beautiful and legitimately good competition – competition not to defeat the other person but just to bring out the best in yourself, which is what, at least from my standpoint, the real definition of competition should be, a striving for self-excellence.

If you look at competition as bringing the best out of yourself, then winning and losing isn't relevant any longer. You want your opponent to do his best because that brings the best out of you. I play tennis a lot, and that's the whole thing in tennis, to give and take. I want my opponent to put his first serve in, because that makes me work harder. Some days I'll go home, and my wife'll say, "How'd you do?" And I'll say, "Horrible, I played lousy." And I might have even won. And some days I'll come home and say I lost but I don't feel bad because we both played really well; it was a good exchange and we both got good exercise. But our society doesn't teach children that. Our society teaches children that you're out to win as opposed to being out to play. It's the same thing about the other side's the enemy. They're the bad guys.

I can remember another instance in high school where, being younger, I used to play in actual games usually just at the closing minutes because I was third-string. I can remember at the very end of a game where our team was getting our pants beat off, and going downfield and trying to block a man and being angry and wanting to hit this guy by throwing myself at him and trying to hit him, and it just happened to be the last play of the game. Right after that happened and the whistle blew, this guy took his helmet off, and he just came up to me immediately and shook my hand, like I'm your best friend. I felt about that big. Here I realized just seconds before I was trying to kill this guy. I'll never forget that as long as I live. Things like that made me realize that I really had some things screwed around backwards in my head. You have to come to those realizations yourself. You're not taught them by your coaches or superiors.

Ted Quant

Convenor of the Survival Coalition, a broad-based umbrella of forty-two different groups in Louisiana, Ted Quant (far left) is very much somebody, and urges others to get together to be "a whole lot of somebodies." He lives in New Orleans with his wife and children.

14

We started the Survival Coalition in 1981, right after Reagan was elected. In February he made his State of the Union address and announced his program for economic recovery. To us, it represented the politics of inhumanity and the economics of barbarism. A total attack on the poor. A shift from human needs to the military, and a shaft for the American people. We called together groups around the state to say we had to do something. We had to organize. That we did not believe there was a mandate for this kind of injustice. And that he had really won with only 25 percent of the vote, of voting-age people. We wanted to organize a counteroffensive for a fair budget and for action to save it. Because what was happening was that people, seeing these cuts, began to say, Oh my God, how am I going to protect my little turf? How am I going to keep my children's program going? How am I going to keep my old age program? Or my day-care program going?

The next point was militarization. That's the third strike against the American people. For every billion dollars of military spending, ten thousand jobs lost to the economy. The fact is that 50 percent of all the money spent in research and development in our country goes to the military. The fact is that any institution that wants to get grants has to first show that it has a military application before it can get it from the government. Then we wonder why we're technologically falling behind in consumer things such as computers, TVs. We look at Japan, and we find that only 2 percent of its national resources go into research and development for military. The rest goes into making better consumer goods.

When we launched this campaign, we started with about twenty-five organizations, then thirty-five organizations, and today we're forty-two organizations in the state of Louisiana. We held a conference to show the impact, and a thousand people came. And that's where we got our first mandate of where we're going.

Then suddenly, I saw the Donahue show. I saw white middle class, formerly middle class individuals, ten couples – one was black – sitting up there. They were all homeless. And they stood before this Donahue crowd and one lady described how she and her husband lost their jobs to the economic crisis. They had run through all of their sub pay and every other kind of pay and unemployment benefits. They had run through their savings and everything else. So then they were begging the landlord not to evict them. Well, the sheriff came and put their furniture out on the street. They put whatever they could carry in their car, and they moved away with nothing. Now, as this impoverished person sat there, one of the ladies in the audience stood up to ask a question. Looked this lady in the eye and said, "I see you got your hair fixed to come on this show." I mean, my heart went out to her. And this lady said, "I fixed my own hair."

The point is, damn her hair; the point is, if she'd come on looking like a bum, they would have said no wonder you can't get a job, you look like a bum. How're you going to look if you're sleeping in your car? If you're shaving in a bathroom of a gas station to try to look good? Keeping your rumpled clothes together when you go to an interview? And when you're hungry and you're scared and you're without good sleep? These are the conditions these people are living under. But what I saw, when that audience pointed and said, You people, you people made these babies, you people should have thought of that before you did this. You people this and you people that.

If you'd have closed your eyes, and it was ten years ago, they would have been all black people up there, and the audience would have been white. And it would have been an expression of their racism as they said, You people this, you people that. I'm going to get you people off my back because I'm going to vote for Ronald Reagan, right? And get you welfare chislers; I've seen the abuses in the breadlines. I've seen the Food Stamp abuses and all this old crap. But all of a sudden, there were some new niggers in our country.

We have to look in other directions for the causes of unemployment, other than scapegoating the victims. These people sat there; they never had been the victims. Their skin color hadn't changed, but their status had. They were called black-tag people, because that's what they call people from Michigan because of their license plates, and they're getting driven out of Texas and beat up because they're seen as taking people's jobs. Here were what I call the new niggers. And the audience, either out of fear, out of . . . sometimes people look at a person that's handicapped or something and are afraid to look at them because it might be them; but somehow or another they make an attack on these people. I don't know if it's a psychological defense mechanism or what, where they had to attack these people almost out of fear because it could happen to them. Rather than saying, Damn, we'll have to change the priorities of government, the victims have to be scapegoated as the cause. Because if you don't scapegoat them as causes, then you've got to ask what are the causes.

One of the blacks up there, a victim, the only black couple, said that the problem in America is that illegal aliens took our jobs. Now once again, with all of the pain they've gone through, the solutions are still simplified answers of attacking another victim. Here is a victim, twice, and he victimizes a third.

I don't understand the abundance that this country has created, this world – we are not in a crisis of poverty. We're not in a crisis where there is too little food or too little housing. We are in a crisis of abundance. And this abundance is the cause of poverty. People are laid off because there are too many cars. Farmers are losing their farms at a thousand per week because there's too much food, yet hundreds of millions of people in the world go hungry. That's a basic, fundamental, kind of contradiction that Martin Luther King spoke about in 1967 before they blew him away, when he said we have solved the problem of production, but we have failed to solve the problem of distribution. The battle for economic justice means some serious reprioritizing, some serious fundamental changes in philosophy and direction, and that's what upsets the hell out of folks.

How people look at themselves and look at other people comes out of the conditions of their lives. In this society, we are conditioned from very early on to have relationships with other people based on manipulation, control and exploitation. And the rewards, the strokes, the reinforcement, a psychological term, are things that are antipeople. That supports this ideology of I-me-my-mine, and what's yours is mine too if I'm slick enough to get it.

What's the number-one best-selling book in America today? *Looking Out for Number One*. Creative selfishness. People on college campuses say, Don't dump that heavy trip on me, baby. I'm going to do something about poverty. I'm going to get an education so I won't be poor. And not understanding the larger structural economic question confronting people, and philosophical questions of whether we're going to feed people when they're hungry because they have a right to exist, to live, by virtue of having been born.

I remember Superfly. Superfly was clean to the max. I mean Superfly was bad. He had the baddest car. He had the baddest suits. He had all of the ladies. He was a dope pusher. He was making it. He was a pimp, a dope pusher, all kinds of bad things. So here come these guys off the street who are about doing something for the community, and they come in to Superfly and say, "Hey brother, you got to do something for the people. We're out here trying to set up this community breakfast program, and we're trying to do this. You gotta give us some money, we got to deal with the system, bro." Superfly looks at 'em and says, "Hey man, when the revolution comes, I'll be for it. In the meantime, get out."

Our society rewards conditions of selfishness. Don't lay a heavy trip on me about somebody else. That ain't my fault they're poor. It ain't my fault there was discrimination. Don't come talkin' to me about no affirmative action. They made their babies anyway, hell, why should I pay for 'em? So don't lay that trip on me. You got your hair fixed for the TV show. Even our relationship with God in the Protestant ethic is an individual thing. God rewards those that's good, and those that's bad got it coming to them.

Justice is an issue. We're in the process of organizing a statewide march for survival and justice on April 16 in Baton Rouge. It's the day after tax day when Americans pay half their income taxes to make new bombs and bullets. According to some statistics I've seen, something around twenty-two to twenty-three thousand dollars is the median income in America. That's hard for me to believe; it sounds like a lot to me, but I guess with two people working maybe that's about right for a family of four.

What that says though is that a family of four pays about five thousand dollars in taxes in that income level. They will pay half of that, $2,500, just for the military. That amounts to $208 a month. Two hundred and eight dollars is a car. Two hundred and eight dollars is a whole lot of commodities that you could buy that would put people back to work. Two hundred and eight dollars a month, or five thousand dollars a year, is a down payment on a new home. It's all these things that the military is robbing us of. Now, what can you do with the tax? You can't eat it, you can't live in it, it won't drive you to work, it does not entertain you, it does not educate your children – and yet half of everything you do goes into that.

I went up to Washington and I talked to my politicians to lobby against militarization and war. And one of them from Louisiana told me, he said, Ted, you don't understand. You don't understand the problem. You see, the Russians can kill 90 percent of us, and we can only kill 50 percent of them, so we've got to catch up. Now, this is one of our elected leaders. One of them high up in the Pentagon said we can win a nuclear war. If we have enough shovels we can dig three-foot holes, put a door over it, put three feet of dirt over it and crawl in it. The secret is the dirt. And we can survive a nuclear war. We have a whole slew of folks who say we have to win the American people to the acceptibility of nuclear war, because it's going to happen. I mean, these folks are not dealing with contingency plans for *if*. They are dealing with *whens*. White supremacy, white chauvinism is so tightly a part of this nation's ideology to a point where people feel that they have a *right* to nuke Iran, nuke Vietnamese, nuke the gooks.

The only thing that I know how to do is organize people around these specific things: winning some small victories, getting our butts kicked, but then sometimes saying, Hey, why did we get our butts kicked? And then saying, What's next? And then keep on keeping on. That's all I know. Like using every means. What did Malcolm say – "By any means necessary"? For example, I'm looking at voting. Look at what's happening with Harold Washington up there. I look at the fact that only one in ten people making less than seven thousand dollars voted in 1978. I look at the fact that in the city of New Orleans there's 91,000 unregistered black voters. I look at the fact that ten million people are on Food Stamps in this country.

We've started with the cheese line. Our coalition goes out everytime there's a cheese distribution; we start registering; we register maybe – here we don't have postcard registration – we've got to take people down. And so if we can register fifty or sixty a day driving them back and forth from off these lines, that's pretty good.

We ask if they're registered, and if they say no, then we say OK, we got a car out here. As soon as you get your cheese, let us drive you down. And we intend to register one hell of a lot of folks here to deal with these political questions. We want to get a black majority in District 2. We have a suit that the Survival Coalition brought, federal court has already heard it, so now we're waiting for a decision. We're doing a lot of good things.

We have got to let people know they can make a difference. An individual, Sister Mary, told me, she said, "I went to prison; I went to jail; I saw prisoners saying how bad they were treated. I said somebody's gotta do something about this. So I went to the priest, and I said, 'Father, somebody's got to do something about this, it's really bad.' The priest said, 'I don't have time.' So I went to someone else, and I said, 'Father, somebody's got to do something about this. The prisoners aren't getting any reading material. They want to get their education, at least get a GED. They have nothing. We've got to do something.' The priest said, 'I don't have time. I've got a lot of things going on.' And so I went through this process of trying to get to the people that I felt could do something. And then it dawned on me: *I* am somebody; *I* have to do something about it." Then she went in there, brought the books, fought with the administrator, got a GED program, and started doing all these various things. And the point of the story to me is that every single person out there in this world is somebody, and together we're a whole lot of somebodies.

Margaret St. Amant

*Widow of a Methodist minister, Margaret St. Amant, here with her daughter and grand-
daughter, lives independently—though near three of her four children and their
families—in Baker, Louisiana, a small town about ten miles from Baton Rouge. Through
a long personal history of pacifism, she speaks with a particular clarity and
forthrightness.*

15

Did you see the president on TV last night? Weird. Expounding on this necessity for doing it up in the satellites, all this high frontier, Star Wars, would only cost, oh, twenty or thirty billion, which would be very reasonable. And of course, that's the first estimate. But it's weird. And I think very fallacious.

Did the thought cross your mind that he may not be all there? Bush was saying on TV tonight, "The president is totally committed to peace." If we can go into this program that he's envisioned, we won't have to fight anybody any more; all we'll do is intercept their weapons and deactivate them, and there won't be any need for any weapons of any kind. We can get rid of all nuclear weapons. They won't be effective any more. This is what he's for. It made a nice-sounding speech, but I don't think it convinced anybody that didn't already agree with him.

Many people believe that our government is deliberately trying to provoke confrontation with Russia. I don't know. I cannot assess Ronald Reagan. He's such a fascinating personality, but I don't know what he's like inside. I know he's at least as old as I am, and that's pretty old. You get pretty well set in your ways by then.

I was in college from '29 to '33. The colleges were so excited by pacifism. There was an immense peace movement in those days, everywhere throughout the United States. The American people were thoroughly against war.

I have a most interesting document in my father's diary in which he traces how the media and the propaganda turned America around in a matter of eighteen months. He says very clearly how everybody in the country was thoroughly opposed to the possibility of war eighteen months ago, and now the whole country is in favor of it. That was when World War II was coming upon us. It's very interesting to read that.

It was done extremely skillfully, and the thing that interests me – I watch everything that goes on with bifocals – is I'm seeing a replay. Everything on TV and radio is a subtle movement toward war mentality, exactly what happened before. And my father in his diary says, "I can understand the young people in the thirties and forties getting duped by this, but how anybody my age who saw it played in World War I can fall for it again, I can't understand." Now, it's replaying again.

My husband, independently of me, was a pacifist, but we were very much attuned to each other in this. In fact, there was a war scare the morning of April 11, 1935, when we were married, and he sat down on the arm of the chair, and said, "You know, that if it comes to war, I'll probably go to prison. You better think well today, and it'll be all right if you decide not to marry me." But I did marry him.

I think we're doing right to focus on the nuclear freeze. As I understand it, the freeze people don't actually expect to achieve it under this administration. They are hoping for a change of administration where it can be achieved. But there's going to come a parting of the ways somewhere because a lot of people under the freeze umbrella really want a strong enough military force in this country to where we are still number one, and that's still militarism.

The time is going to have to come when the opposite of peace is not war, when the opposite of peace is unpeace. And unpeace is the whole business of having to be number one, of having to control, of being able to control world markets. A lot of freeze supporters will not go with the folks who are looking for the opposite of unpeace, the actual goodwill, being able to cooperate with and wish for the success of peoples whose policies are different from ours, whose history is different from ours, whose ways of doing things are different from ours, who offer something besides violence with which to run this world.

I read somewhere the other day that in the declassified papers of former presidents, every one of them said in private, We know that there's no Russian threat. We use it. A lot of it resides in the economy. It's part and parcel of the administration's economic program, to give aid to the big manufacturers. There's money in armaments, and we're selling them and giving them away wherever we can.

I think people have been scared to death, deliberately. I've not read this anywhere, but it's crossed my mind that what we have really been doing in building up our armaments, our nuclear armaments, was inviting Russia to do likewise, hoping to cause the complete collapse of the Russian economy. We've come very close to causing our own, but that would be a nice painless way of destroying Russia.

We've got to do something about the immense nuclear buildup. We've got to call a halt first, and I use a very homely illustration. The president says we're going to get rid of some of the nuclear weapons, and I say you've got two grown men with two big bathtubs and the water going full stream, and they're arguing over whether to dip out with a two-quart dipper or a

three-pint dipper. And somebody yells and says, "Turn off the water!" And
if we don't turn off the escalation of building more nuclear weapons, what
we do in the way of reduction is ridiculous. In fact, the president has no
notion of reduction whatsoever. His whole plan is to fool the American
people. The Rusians know it and laugh in his face. They're not fools. It's
plumb silly. There's no way to reduce nuclear arms in any siginificant way
without turning off the faucets.

Again, I see this with bifocals. We had disarmament conference after
disarmament conference before '41. Each one learned a little bit more
about what the other side had so they could go home and make some more.
We had a fabulous book in those days, called *Merchants of Death*, that
exposed the great munitions makers and the money that was involved in it.
Ask me why people want peace and are preparing for war – because
there's money in it. And this administration has sold more weaponry and
given more weaponry and appropriated more weaponry than ever before.
We've been doing it for years now, just spreading it over the face of the
earth.

The thing Eisenhower said – "the pervasive control of our government,
economy and culture by the military-industrial complex" – was at the time
of his administration the most serious indictment yet issued. His warning
is a hundredfold more pertinent today, except it should be called the
"military-industrial-labor-university complex." Now, it's all wrung in there
together. The frightening this about it is, whenever you really move closer
to war, you lose democracy. You go into a semidictatorship. What you fight
for, you've already lost. And you don't know for sure that you'll get it back.

Take the history of the Christian church. You have about 150 years of
pacifism, and then they begin to protect themselves. Then you have Con-
stantine as emperor in 300-something AD; the whole thing changes and
you've got the theory of a just war. Every war has always been just on both
sides, according to who's telling it. The Germans in World War I wore hel-
mets that said In God We Trust. The Kaiser had family prayers every
morning. They thought they were fighting for right. Every side always
feels they're fighting for right.

There's no way to save the human race in a nuclear age, unless, like Ein-
stein said, unless we're willing to say that love is strong enough to change
people. If you accept the risk. I'm sitting here in a comfortable house and
not on my way to jail, but Gandhi went to jail, Martin Luther King went to
jail, and a great many other people have been to jail. Who knows? We may
go too. You cannot defend yourself into peace.

This business requires faith. Keep renewing your faith. If God still believes in us, still believes that we and the world He so loved are redeemable, then we can believe in ourselves and others and the possibility of abolishing nuclear armament, and all war munitions, too, when it comes to actually going forward on the business of risk. For the sake of peace. Which means undiscourageable good will. Not counting their trespasses against them. Not trying to get even. One of the real whammies in that passage from the Sermon on the Mount is that we are to do good to those that hate us and pray for those that are spiteful.

So much of theology has been tit-for-tat theology, we've even built our whole theology of hell on tit for tat. Jesus says that's not God. God is forgiveness and transforming and unconditional love. I don't love you because you are good. I don't love you because you love me. I don't love you necessarily because it's going to do any good. I love you because love is right. That's where my pacifism comes from.

The greatest component of the power of love is willingness to risk. That's what makes power. Expendability. Risking. This is what Jesus did. He said, If any man loves his life, he will lose it. If he loses his life, he shall gain it. To me, the whole matter of saving this world from destroying itself is going to have to rest on those who are willing to accept the thesis that you don't do it safely.

I was at a preachers and preachers' wives supper that I get in on still. I was sitting beside a very fine black minister, and something was said about war. And he said flatly, as most anybody will tell you, "Human nature being what it is, we'll never have peace." I said, "Sir, if you and I had sat together two hundred years ago, we would have both said, 'Human nature being what it is, we'll never get rid of slavery. It's been with us since the beginning of time. There's no way to get rid of it.'" And I said, "God works through human beings to change social institutions." We've got a lot of things wrong, and our race relationships are not right, but we do not have the institution of slavery. And the time will come when we will not have the institution of war.

J. R. Grisham

J. R. Grisham is a Methodist minister who allegedly retired in 1980 at "age sixty-nine years." But he has more energy and enthusiasm and projects than many six-year-olds. Around Tupelo, in northeastern Mississippi, J. R. is an effective force for anything from lobbying Jamie Witten (D., 1st District), powerful chairman of the House Appropriations Committee, to speaking out on all those matters in which he believes. Which are quite a few.

16

I retired in 1980, May, age sixty-nine years. I just have more to do than I can get done. I can't understand people retiring. I'm real involved in Common Cause. We have two delegates from each congressional district, and I'm one from the 1st District, and very involved in that. I'm also involved to an extent in Bread for the World, and in Target Tupelo.

I'm going to speak to the ladies group at the First Methodist Church week after next, and I've decided to load for them before I get in there. What I'm going to do, I'm going to go down and see how many books they got in their Library on the nuclear problem. The first thing I'm going to do is interrogate them on their reading and studying on the issue. What have you read? Have you read any books on it? See, I'm going to put them on the spot before they get at me. How can you speak out on anything that you haven't done any studying on? I've decided I don't know if they're going to be ready for me, but I'm going to be ready for them! What I'm saying is we've got to be wise as serpents in dealing with this thing because the opposition deals in cliches, and that's always difficult to deal with, cliches. "Get the government off your back" is terribly hard to deal with. I tell them if Reagan wanted to get the government off people's backs, now he's got the government in women's wombs. Isn't that very interesting?

We've got a strange development. You take the pro-life group, for example. All right, now what do they say about capital punishment? What do they say about war? That's all right to kill 'em that way. I see something in this abortion thing I've never heard a person mention. I think what's behind it is this conservative group is trying to get back at the Supreme Court because of their decision on civil rights. They won't come out and tell you that, but that's what they're trying to do. They're mad at the Supreme Court because of civil rights, and you can't get elected down here in the South if you blast that. So what they do, is they take this abortion route.

We know that we can destroy – that America and Russia have enough now that they can destroy everything on this earth. We got one submarine – I heard a congressman say this – we got one submarine that can destroy, literally destroy, Russia. One. And yet we need more. More of everything. That's all Weinberger and those fellas know is more. You think about this argument over whether we're going to have a 4 percent increase in the defense budget or 10 percent. Lord of mercy knows. It ought to be a 50 percent decrease, but this is the argument. It shows you the power these people have.

I think of the audacity of this arms buildup that we're in. It doesn't make sense any way you can look at it. If we can destroy Russia and Russia can destroy us, and if we can destroy everything in the world, and if we've got one submarine that can destroy everything in Russia, why do we need more? You can only say it's an issue that you can frighten people over. And that's what Reagan's doing. I don't know what it is, but it goes back to this old thing that if you wrap it up in the flag you can do anything. There it is. Just wrap it up in the flag. Patriotism, see. But it's awfully difficult to answer these things. You just have to keep working at it.

I am reading *The Buck Starts Here,* a fine little book. It starts with you. It doesn't stop here, it starts with you. It's easy to pass this big buck off to God or to our denominational peace groups. It's hard to face up to the fact that each of us as an individual holds part of the nuclear war buck. As one poster says, "In a democracy, we all push the button."

If Reagan had been defeated in 1980, and Carter had been elected, what would the Republicans be saying about Jimmy Carter? They'd want impeachment, that's what they'd want. A man that came in to balance the budget by 1983, he's going to balance the budget? We've got the largest deficit, more than all the deficits we've ever had combined. And we're spending on something that's not productive; it's bound to come back to haunt us.

I don't see how the man—he's a shrewd operator, and he's got lots of money behind him. That's the reason Adolph Hitler was able to come to power. With money. Germany got behind him; the Krupp steel mills, the industrialists got behind him. It was on television the other day, I didn't know this, Henry Ford backed him, one of our millionaires over here. I never heard that before. I don't know if it's true or not. But I *do* know what happened over there. What I'm so deeply concerned about is our people. It's like Rip Van Winkle—we've gone to sleep for twenty years, if there's anything left in twenty years. We're asleep.

The opossum, as you know, is a prehistoric animal. It should never have lived over into this time. It's prehistoric. Well, war is prehistoric. It's not for modern man. It's prehistoric. And yet we still carry this over. I think this goes back to Joe McCarthy and Richard Nixon. This communism thing, what they did, they jumped on a little thing of guilt by association. Communism became the whipping boy. And Richard Nixon was elected on this.

He identified his opponent as being ... see, rabbits, rabbits eat carrots and man eats carrots, therefore, man is a rabbit. That's syllogistic thinking. It fools people. And you can fool a lot of people. We've had a whole long history of that through Joe McCarthy and then through Richard Nixon, and there's still this pattern.

I don't think we have done a very good job in America of really educating our people to the point of critical thinking. I think it's been muddled thinking. And we've had it at the highest levels. A person with not very much intelligence would realize it. We're not educated on how to think through a problem. Give a little cliche.' What you gonna do with the Russians? That's the ultimate of our thinking. And yet we are supposed to be a highly enlightened society.

I want to have a lot of faith. That's the hope. The Lord is in control of this thing; he hasn't lost control of it. But I also know he's given us free will. We can have a First World War, Second World War; we can have a Third World War, if we decide to do it. He's not going to come down and save us. He gave us free will. Thank goodness I have a good many opportunities to go into churches. You can drop a lot of these things in churches. I very often ask the pastor if he's had this film in his church; I know he hasn't but let him tell me. You ought to have this film, *The Last Epidemic*, in your church, I say to them. I want to quote from it. If we don't solve this problem, nothing else matters, because you won't have anything left to solve.

Chuck Guenther

*Long an active supporter of the St. Louis Economic Conversion Project, which counsels
people working in the defense industries to consider other areas of employment, Chuck
Guenther was himself an engineer with McDonnell-Douglas. With two young children,
Chuck and his wife know first hand the risks involved in real bread-and-butter change.
They have also learned the hope that comes with it. St. Louis has a particularly large
and diverse defense industry. Besides McDonnell-Douglas, the largest such employer
in the area, it includes the world corporate headquarters of General Dynamics, the
largest defense contractor anywhere, and over five hundred smaller firms dependent
to varying degrees on related work. Not paradoxically, St. Louis also has a diverse
and determined peace community, composed of clergy and laity alike.*

17

I worked for McDonnell Douglas for fifteen years. I was an engineer, mostly in flight tests, designed instruments. I helped in the operational day-to-day maintenance of instrumentation for test airplanes. I spent a year out at Edwards Air Force Base working on upgrading a so-called improved model of the F-4 Phantom. I also spent a couple of years working on ground equipment that is used to maintain the F-15 aircraft.

I guess I did about half a dozen jobs that were very highly specialized in some way or another. It's a little hard to describe what I did. But basically I had a very very small amount of responsibility for a particular technical area of weapons systems.

Back in 1966, when I started, the Vietnam War was heating up. If you went to work in the defense industry you would receive a deferment. In many cases that resulted in people not being drafted, never being drafted for that war.

Salary is another big consideration, too. Another reason, very attractive for engineers, is being able to work with good, modern, up-to-date equipment, and working on state-of-the-art technology. These things are attractions in the defense industry because that's where the money is. They can afford to buy the equipment for these contracts.

There is a competitive drive to keep up with the technology, especially in electronics, to be able to stay on top of it, stay technically sharp. In electronics, and especially in military electronics, there's a rapid turnover of usefulness of technology. Things become obsolete so fast it's very difficult to keep up. If you can work your way in one job and be successful, you'll be rewarded with another project with a little more responsiblity and be able to stay sharp that way. My approach was to try to stay technically sharp and competent because I wanted to be an engineer for the rest of my life.

In many cases, it's the best — at least it's the best-paid technical talent — that goes into the defense industry. There are very, very high priorities placed on projects. I remember a project I was working on where we decided that we needed another $100,000 computing system for testing our VF-18 aircraft. We decided we needed it in a few months. The sales rep from the computer company told us that the normal delivery cycle was

about a year, but we could have ours within a few months because there
were other orders, placed for instance by automobile companies, for the
same computer system, and they said we could have one of theirs simply
by invoking a national defense priority, and we actually did that. We
butted in line, grabbed the computer that we wanted, meanwhile putting
off the autmobile company which probably needed it. And I would suspect
that their need was a lot more rational than ours. If the truth were known,
we didn't have to have this computer system at all, certainly not for
national defense.

My political awakening really began with the Watergate scandals.
Watergate really shook my political beliefs to the foundations, just turned
me around. Also my children were growing up, were four or five years old,
and were starting to ask me the usual questions about what does Dad do
at work, and I found it difficult to describe what I was doing. Partly
because it was specialized, but also because it was related to applications
that I didn't often want to think about. Fighter airplanes, fighter bombers.
A lot of the things I did were associated with bomb drop tests, and until I
started looking into it, I didn't even realize that some of these bomb drop
tests were tactical nuclear weapons, napalm, things like that. I just viewed
these things as objects that were dropped off the airplane, and the tests
were designed to make sure they dropped off and didn't hit the airplane.

Then I found out about the MX missile. Our company didn't have any
contracts with it, but I remember reading about it, around '77 or '78, when
President Carter was proposing the roadbed-type MX missile. It was supposed to be such a large project that it would take 30 to 40 percent of the
country's concrete capacity for several years to build, and might have
turned out to be the largest project ever undertaken by the human race. I
remember that really got to me when I heard about it. I was thinking how
useless that was, what a waste.

I more and more believe that with the increasing world population and
decreasing fossil fuels, people are going to have to be more oriented
towards building things which are needed in their own communities, and
needed by other people. Not build things simply to offend other countries,
or destroy them, or threaten them.

I was concerned by an article in this morning's *Globe Democrat*, a revelation by Jack Anderson where he has documented proof that the United
States has, at least on paper, considered first strike scenarios on the
Soviet Union, where the MX missile or the new Trident missiles are going
to play a vital role.

I used to think the whole military-industrial complex was a form of
middle class welfare, but in recent months I've come to think of it as

organized crime. Legal organized crime. Glom onto all these resources and fan hatred of other countries in order to get to those resources, in order to continue this madness.

I think the increased military budgets, for instance, are locking into place a lot of things that can't be undone very easily or very quickly. In other words, we're locking in place weapons systems for years to come. I saw a lot of that at McDonnell Douglas, too – advanced planning groups that are working on new weapons systems for the 1990s and beyond.

Another thing I'm afraid of is the increased amount of secrecy that's going on. On April 15, which was tax day, there was an announcement that General Dynamics received a new contract award for a Stealth Air Launch Cruise missile. This is using Stealth technology to decrease the radar visibility of the Cruise missile, and the amount of the contract award was kept secret. It was classified information, not available to the public. Saying it's none of our business how much money they're spending on this new technology, on this new weapons system. Very dangerous.

The main focus of the St. Louis Economic Conversion Project is to simply educate people about the need for conversion, conversion in a peaceful direction at a time when there's an increasing amount of actual conversion taking place towards war-making industry because of the increased military budget. And trying to keep alive the hope and also the truth that conversion is not something that's impractical or pie-in-the-sky dreams; it's something that's very, very possible. It simply takes political will to do it.

The guys going to their jobs at General Dynamics or McDonnell Douglas or one of the five hundred smaller companies in the area that receive contracts from the government, I'm sure a lot of them would talk to you first about the Soviet threat, how we have to deal with that. But I think that is a mask that really covers fears about their own jobs. In other words, it's a good excuse. And the propaganda that's going on is helping to provide that excuse. When you approach them about conversion, a lot of people become fearful about conversion of their own jobs. They want to know that if there was a conversion process going on, they would want to be absolutely sure that they in particular would get one of those new jobs, be able to learn it, and be able to do the job. And so they are caught up in the old security game that a bird in the hand is worth two in the bush. And that this is where they get their check right now, and right now is what's important, especially with high unemployment.

I think people are beginning to think in terms of not only attainment of more material things and goods, but quality of life, and being able to enjoy things, enjoy sports, enjoy children. There are people right now as a result of the current economic depression we're in that are having to live with less income. And they're finding that's not so bad. We're one of those families. I think we may have to give up some of those material things that we now pursue in order to rid the planet of the threat of war.

My wife has gone to work. She's had a full-time job for the last year or so, and I've been part-time teaching, hoping to get a full-time position; basically I'm drifting from part-time teaching job to part-time teaching job. But I'm finding it rewarding, working with people. At Forest Park Community College, I'm in the science and technology department, and I teach part-time for the math department as well as the electronics technology department. And I also teach computer programming courses.

Right now, I'm in the midst of contemplating being in a civil disobedience action. That's occupying a lot of my thoughts the last few days. It's going to take place in St. Louis this coming Monday. I see it as something that's more and more necessary, people demanding that their governments obey international laws. And also things which may not have been codified into international law, but that are just right and true and moral.

My family, too, is going to be there in support. We've talked it over as a family, and the kids were very insistent that they wanted to get out of school to be there and watch dad get arrested and carried off.

In St. Louis my impression is civil disobedience used to be mainly employed as a tactic by religious people, nuns and priests, people with some kind of real umbrella over them. Now I think that support system is extending into the larger community. More ordinary people with jobs—myself, and I think of Mark Shue, Carolyn Stevens and others—are planning to risk arrest. I think it's the feeling that there is a support system extending beyond the churches.

I can't help but think about what kind of jobs and roles my children will be playing, too. They're eleven and twelve years old right now, and I certainly hope that they have a more open set of choices than today. I hope for instance that they aren't drafted into a war. I hope that they don't . . . even if they're not drafted, I hope they don't go to work in the defense industry, for instance, to avoid the draft, like I did. I hope there will be useful things for them to work on. I know that there's useful needs and things; it's just a matter of orienting our society to fulfill those needs rather than maximizing profits.

Dorothy Armbruster

Whether boycotting a liquor chain in support of farm workers or quietly spinning at her wheel during a sit-in at General Dynamics headquarters, Dorothy Armbruster long has been a gentle but powerful presence in the St. Louis peace community. In her spare time she's raised two families of adopted children, five in the first generation, four in the second.

18

For the last couple of years, I've not been able to be as active as I'd like. I'm so caught up lately in mundane family involvements, community involvements, my parents' health, that sort of thing. I feel these take so much time that I'm not able to be broadly involved or really commit myself like I'd like to. I wrestle with these limitations a lot.

Over the years I've been so fortunate to be involved here. At the time of the Vietnam War, a group of us were trying to get us out of the war, and as an outgrowth of that, CALC came into being in St. Louis, as it did all over the country. And just through a few little contacts with people that I happen to have a lot of respect for . . . when I look back on it, I realize how much I got out of it, because it led me into all kinds of understanding and opportunity to meet all kinds of people.

It's been such an inspiration to be around people that felt secure in their sense of values and their willingness to allow you to try to find your goals and ways.

I think, once you start to get any perception of injustices in the world, whether it's racial injustice, sexist injustice, economic injustice, whatever, then things begin to snowball. And you find that it's all part of the same picture.

I think the trigger in my particular situation was way back in high school. There was a teacher that I had who was supposed to teach chemistry, and she taught the tragedy of racial prejudice instead. This was in St. Louis in 1939 and 1940.

Being able to make these connections, I feel that maybe some of it sifts through me into the upper middle class community I live in. I think there's some value in having the opportunity to introduce different ways of thinking about lifestyles here, and translating it to people. For example, in the schools. When they see me walk into the school, they know something's up.

I think the strongest element in St. Louis that got going was the Farm Workers Movement. A lot of the same people connected with the Catholic Worker Movement and CALC are now working on this, working together. We're part of a network all over the country in support of their efforts. We organize local boycotts here in St. Louis in order to have the growers in

California negotiate. For instance, we boycotted a liquor chain, 905, because of their limes, and we are a presence there just like we are at General Dynamics.

I really feel it's more of an economic thing than anything else, as far as the power. And I think it's very difficult to tap that because we're so tied into the capitalistic system. And it's affecting the economy in our own country, and it's affecting the economy of the world. That's why I think that the resolutions that we have brought up to the stockholders' meetings of these particular companies that are munitions, arms manufacturers, are so important.

The idea of economic conversion is a tremendous factor, because otherwise we're doing injustice to the people who work for the companies. Because they're afraid of their jobs, and they should be afraid. We've got to think about how do we address this so that they don't suffer because of it. There's no reason why they should be the ones who bear the brunt of it. The resolutions we have presented at the shareholders' meetings have always included that kind of thing, having planning for and getting under-way an economic conversion in that company. The needs are there.

People are insecure in their own neighborhoods. But again, a lot of that's an economic thing, because we have people who are without jobs. And if you're without a job, you're without self-esteem, you're without money that you need. You have time on your hands. What do you do with the time? That's not developing people's human resources, their human capabilities.

Just now the St. Louis budget was cut back, and a lot more people will be without jobs. That's unhealthy. I would say that all of that is *undoing*. That's not security. I don't see where our country is secure at all. We can have all the arms in the world, but if that kind of situation exists, we live in a terrible time.

I think so many of us, who are people who have power because we have money, don't see that enough. We are just divorced from the everyday lives of people who don't have it.

Ken Graham

An unusually circuitous road has led Ken Graham through several vocations, and Vietnam. Currently he is a physician and medical school teacher. Similarly, his faith has wandered. Born into a Unitarian family, his spirit has carried him far. Roman Catholic in practice, and acknowledged by many in Tulsa as almost single-handedly responsible for the Catholic Worker House there, Ken is feeling his interest in Buddhism slowly returning. Somehow it all seems to fit.

19

In '64 was when I graduated from college, and Vietnam was just starting to warm up. I decided that – I'd been on college deferment – I really didn't want to get involved with this Vietnam thing, so I took a couple of years of graduate school. My wife taught elementary school, and I went to a couple years of graduate school, and then it was 1966. By that time, Vietnam was really getting to go, so I went in and really took to it. I was raised in a very conservative family. My father was a hero of sorts in World War II, and I really took to the military. Really enjoyed it. I'm a person who likes a lot of structure, and so I fit into that real well. I joined the Marine Corps, for God's sake. Here I had a master's degree; I didn't have to do that. I could've gone into other services. I didn't even have to go in the infantry, let alone the Marine Corps, but it was just one of those things – you can be your own worst enemy. I think it was just part of my nature.

I never really understood until just recently where – I had a flashback to the Vietnam experience six or seven months ago – where I began to realize why I joined the Marine Corps. Why did I volunteer immediately to go to Vietnam once I got through training? About six, seven months ago I just woke up in the middle of the night. I hadn't had any real problems since Vietnam. Trouble sleeping when I first came back, a few nightmares, those kinds of things. Just for a few months, nothing much. Pretty much I had worked my way through all of that. I knew I still carried a lot of guilt. I used to compulsively cry every time I thought about it very much. But I still didn't feel like it was that big of a deal until I woke up in the middle of the night seven months ago. I started screaming and yelling and grabbed my wife's head and pushed her down in the bed and told her, "Get down, get down." Screaming, yelling, really freaked out. And my poor wife, of course, had no idea what was going on. I continued to give orders for about thirty minutes; we were having a fire fight. Then I started crying. And I started crying because of all the guys that got killed.

Actually, in my platoon, I was in the field for about seven months and then I was transferred to the rear, to Division CP, but in the seven months I was in the field no one actually got killed. And we were in constant contact, daily contact. Had a few guys shot; nobody killed. But two weeks after I left the platoon – and I jumped at the first chance to get out – about half the platoon was killed. By the new lieutenant, I always said. Kind of blamed him because he was a brand new lieutenant and didn't know his way around. And I felt like always that these guys would not have died had I stayed in the platoon. So that was always my major guilt. I started crying and asking for Hadley, my bazooka man – he was just someone I was very close to, just a simple Iowa farm boy. I always felt like he probably hated me because I abandoned the platoon and got all these guys killed. Anyway, then I proceeded to cry for about two hours, middle of the night, just begging these guys, and especially Hadley to forgive me for abandoning the platoon and all this sort of stuff.

Obviously the next day I knew I had a problem. So I contacted the local Vet Center and went down, went through a few counseling sessions, did some role-playing. This guy had Hadley come in and sit down in a chair and me talk to him, that kind of stuff. It was really very, very good, and I'm still kind of working through all the fallout of that myself. Being a physician, I'm constantly doing that with other people, but it's very hard to suddenly find yourself in such need, and suddenly the role is reversed.

The fellow who was doing the counseling was also a combat vet. He was a sergeant over there. Asked me to think of some good things about Vietnam. What was good? What did it do good? And I said, I don't come at this that way. I said, You're approaching it wrong with that question. I said, It's evil, we shouldn't have been there. I didn't believe that, of course, when I went over there. But he said no, I still want you to do it. And I said well, there isn't any way that I can conceive of anything good in my experience. But I thought about it, and I did come up with a couple things that I hoped were not a perverse way of seeing good.

The one main point was that I was being true to my beliefs and to my system and to my understanding. At that time, I thought it was the right thing to do. I believed it was right, I believed I needed to do this for my country, I believed I needed to do it for my parents. That I owed it to my country to go do this thing. I don't believe that way now. I owe it to my country *not* to do those kinds of things. But at the time I was still being true to myself.

The other thread was that I'd been lied to. It was as if your parents had lied to you, that's the exact expression I used. My parents lied to me, my country lied to me, my president lied to me. I got over there and saw all these things in terms of trying to save the world for democracy. It wasn't happening. We were over there fighting for the people of South Vietnam. And it's readily apparent to me, that it was a surrogate war. In other words, because of our xenophobia about communism, we want to fight communism in all those little places around the world. And that was just one way of doing it, that one particular time. The old domino theory. We don't want to fight the communists here, so we're going to fight them there.

When I got back from Vietnam I was spiritually lost; I was just spiritually adrift. I became real interested in Buddhism because I had gotten interested in the martial arts. I got interested in the martial arts because I could not control my temper. I would fly off the handle. I was over thirty at this point, and I was getting in fights. That was ridiculous. I just was a pretty lost soul.

I'm not really involved with changing the world any more. That was real important to me at one time. Mother Theresa said something a few years ago that has had a tremendous impact on me in terms of kind of getting me to understand myself. I hate to reduce things down to one-liners, but her statement that God does not call us to be successful but rather to be faithful – that's turned me around so much because at so many different times I see people burning themselves out. And I always think, In the peace movement we're trying to be successful, and if we're not converting people, if we're not saving the country, the world, whatever, then somehow it's failure.

Friday was my last day of school; I've got two and half months off this summer. I haven't had that since my school teaching days, before '75. Medical school, first two years of practice, all those things are very dehumanizing, I would even use the word psychotic; I am just now barely recovering psychologically and spiritually from that experience. And so, this summer represents to me the first time that I've kind of got it all back together in terms of feeling comfortable with myself, in terms of feeling whole.

I'm going to Boston on Thursday to visit a friend. I haven't been to the Vietnam Memorial in Washington, DC. We're going to spend two days there. He's a vet too. I'm going to go back up to Boston and spend a week there visiting, going to visit PSR [Physicians for Social Responsibility] and other stuff. But mainly, this summer is just to kind of heal a lot of old wounds. I need to do more with the Vietnam thing. I need to discover again who I am.

Yes, it's going to be tough, but I'm really looking forward to it. I'm going to go find Hadley's name. That's the most important thing. When I see his name, I don't know what's going to happen to me. I know I'm going to break down, but I just think that will be, to see his name there, somehow I'm hoping that that will be a healing experience. That is my wish and my hope. I don't think I really have any choice.

Eloy Ramos

Answering Bishop Matthiesen's challenge that those employed in the defense industries search out alternative careers is one notable person, Eloy Ramos. To answer his bishop's urging—and to do God's will—takes tremendous courage with a wife and seven kids. Eloy wrestled with the decision for several years before quitting his job with the U.S. Department of Energy's Pantex facility, the final assembly point for all nuclear warheads in the United States.

20

We grew up, all grew up on a farm, all the brothers and sisters. My father was a peanut farmer in San Antonio.

When I was a little boy, maybe five years old, hardly walking, I was working in the fields. Hoeing peanuts and black-eyed peas. We planted a little bit of that, and corn and everything. I go back and remember those beautiful days. You can go back to the days when you worked with your dad. I remember the sun real hot. There's a lot of sand over there. A lot of white sand, and I had no shoes. My feet – I'd try to be hiding from the sun. The sand gets real hot, and I'd try to cover my feet, step in the weeds so it wouldn't be so hot. In the peanuts, when they were big, I could hide my feet under the leaves. Shade.

And I would look up at the sky, and I would hear about the people that worked for the government, how easy they had it. There were about three or four bases out there, and a lot of civil service employees. I would look at the sky, and I would talk to God and say, "God, if you ever give me a job, an easy job like that where I'd have security, and it'll be easy like the people out there working in these bases, I would really be grateful to You." Here I am, my feet on fire, and I would just look at the sky and just think and just talk to God.

I grew up and got married when I was sixteen years old. My wife was sixteen also. My oldest son was born when I was seventeen years old. And it was real hard for me because I couldn't find a job. I was so young. So I had to work on the farm picking cotton for a couple of years until I was old enough to find a job, a regular job. We struggled, my wife and I, and finally I got a job – what I'm doing now, in a fence company, working for Allied Fence Company down in San Antonio.

My brother, my oldest brother, was a radio announcer out there in San Antonio. He knew some people working in the base, where they were also assembling some nuclear weapons. He told me, "Why don't you go and apply for a job; I've got some friends out there. They might be able to set you up." And so I did, and within a year and a half they called me. I never thought they'd call me because I didn't have . . . I had a ninth-grade education. I didn't think they were going to call me. So I was surprised when they wrote me a letter stating they wanted me to go and take a physical. I was really thrilled about that. I couldn't believe it. Unbelievable!

They gave me a physical, and in about a month they called me. I couldn't believe it that morning. I thought, Well, they told me out there, they said we don't call everybody who we give a physical. If you're all right, we'll put you on the list. The chances are that we might call you, but don't get your hopes up high. So anyway, I said, "No, that's too good to be true." I couldn't believe it.

A couple of months after that, or a month, they gave me a call. I was working for Diamond Fence Company, and they happened to call that morning I was in the office. I picked up the phone and they said, "This is the base, and we want to talk to Eloy Ramos," and I said, "This is Eloy Ramos." And they said – it was a Thursday, I think – they said, "We want you to report to work Monday." I thought, Boy, they don't give me enough time to tell my boss here that I'm quitting. I said I was thinking about giving him a notice. I didn't know I was going to get the job. They said, "Well, if you want the job, we need you Monday." I said, "So, I'll be out there Monday." I wasn't going to let something like that go by. Once in a lifetime, you know. So anyway, I told my boss, and he didn't like it too good. He said, well, he said, I guess, if you must go, you must go. But they liked me pretty good at the fence company. I hated to be that way, because the guy I was working for, he was giving me all the gas in my car, and he was paying me real good, too. They liked me.

A lot of people, when they heard that I was working out at the base, a lot of people that had high school educations, or college, they asked me, "How did you get out there?" The kids who used to know me in school, who used to laugh at me because I had patches on my blue jeans and overalls, when they found that I was working on Medina base, they can't believe that. I said, "Well, I went out there and I applied for a job, and I was called." They said, "We applied for a job out there and all over them bases, and we haven't been called."

Time went on, and they shut the plant door there. About a year I worked out there, and they said we're going to shut this plant. So about six months before they shut the plant down they started putting up notices for jobs in other areas of the United States where they assembled the metal weapons. They had about three or four places where I could choose. And I said, "Well, I wanted the nearest place, where I can be near to Mom and Dad."

I always was real close to Mom and Dad. Dad passed away about a year ago, but I'm real close to Mom now, more so that she's by herself now. I've got a brother staying with her, but he doesn't talk, he can't talk.

Anyway, I chose Amarillo. It was January 28 I got here. There was snow out here, a lot of snow, and I told my wife, I said, "Girl, I don't think we're going to make it here. There's too much snow." But we finally got adjusted to the place. I can't say that I like it. I never have liked this place because I was raised on a farm where there was a lot of water, a lot of trees, and all the time it was pretty. And the bad thing is that I'm away from my brothers and sisters and Mom. I really miss them. I never have gotten used to this area.

I remember back to the farm, back when I was a little kid, as far as I can remember, it was World War II, when my uncle was at the war. He was fighting. I used to see my grandma. She used to pray every night. She was a lady with a lot of faith. And I would lay down in bed, or I would sit, watch her, and I would think about God. I would wonder the sacrifice she would do, kneeling there for maybe an hour, half an hour every night.

She always stayed near us. I would see her do that every night, pray for her sons to come back from the war. She was a beautiful lady to the kids. She was the most beautiful lady that I have ever known in this world. She was a real kind person, and she had nothing bad to say about anybody. She was always reading the Bible and giving us advice about obeying parents and what God wants of us and everything. I think right there she opened me in the mind – not right then, but I started wondering about God then – when I was a kid.

Anyway, I was working here for a few years, and I started getting into the church, studying the Bible, and I started thinking. As I worked out there I often thought about what God wanted for his people, for his creation. Before I left the plant, people used to criticize me a little bit about what I was doing. And I said, "Well, this is what I was called to do. And believe me, it's not easy."

They would call me . . . Well, since when did you become a communist? Since when . . . I said, "Well, I've been here in this shop for many years now, trying to please you people. And I was never disrespectful to any of you. I didn't abuse any of you. I was a shop steward, and there never was any injustice. I would see when you would complain to me, I would take your complaint to the administration building and we would straighten it out." I said, "You never see me out here abusing women or anything like that, or my fellow workers or anything like that. I respect my superiors in everything. And you stand there now and tell me that I am a communist. You don't know what I'm going through, but I can tell you why you're calling me that. Because you want to justify your staying here.

"What is it?" I said, "Why do you want to hurt me? Do you want to make me feel bad? It's not easy. You cannot say that I was lazy or that I was any thing that I mentioned a while ago. Well, why do you call me that? You know that I love God. You've asked me a lot of times, Why, why are you doing this? And I've quoted you the Bible a lot of times, and you don't understand." And I said, "Well, if you don't understand, understand the Bible, I can tell you I'm leaving here because – simply because I love you and I know your family, and I love the future generations. Do you understand that?" And they'd say, "Well, I guess; I don't know."

God is tired of us just saying . . . God is tired of us coming out on TV and saying how beautiful He is and how beautiful He is and how beautiful we love our brother. God is tired of the radio when he hears us saying how beautiful God, and how beautiful God is this and God is that. God wants to see . . . He wants to see . . . He's tired of that. He has just about given up on us, I said. We bring Him material things; He doesn't want that. He wants our love for our brother. This is what God wants.

The people don't care one way or another anymore, I think. If you quit, fine; if you stay, fine. As long as they're making a living, it doesn't matter one way or another. This is my fear for the future.

I know that God is with me, and I know God tells me. It helps a lot. Before I quit the plant I said, "I'm not going to look for another job. I'm going to quit without having another job." I made a title, just joking, I said, "My departure from Pantex is a Journey in Search for the People of God. The people of God, what are they going to answer when they see me? Are they going to answer? Are they going to help me? What are they going to do?"

I didn't know what I was going to do in the winter. I was terrified: What am I going to do in the wintertime? It was one of the hardest winters, and I had money saved up, and I didn't even use it. I told my wife, can you see that? God will provide for us. God is here, and He'll help us. I said all we have to do is believe in Him and do the things that He wants us to do. He's been good to us.

Frank Duncan

Frank Duncan, rancher and retired ophthalmologist, lives with his wife Estelle in Amarillo, Texas, although his heart is on the ranch. Amarillo, the largest city in the Texas Panhandle, continues to grow and expand, and is also known around the world for the Pantex facility, the final assembly point for all nuclear warheads in the United States; it is operated by the Pantex Corporation for the U. S. Department of Energy.

21

Texas has always been a very conservative area, and people have habitually given total confidence to government decisions. And it's very difficult for them to view with suspicion any governmental action. They accept most governmental decisions and policies without any question. It's customary and habitual to do that, and they pride themselves in being super-patriotic because of that way of behaving. Anything the government does is "our government right or wrong." And they don't feel like they should interfere with the decision of the ones who they perceive as being the policymakers.

I began to perceive that, after they developed atomic weaponry, that decisions were being made without any consultation with the electorate. We were not even informed of the decisions, policies. If we were informed of them, it was done very casually, and after the fait accompli. It had already been done, and no one had any particular opportunity to do anything about it.

For instance, the average citizen has no idea where all these weapons are stored, the sites of the silos, where they're directed. Who controls them, how they're controlled. We have no idea about that at all. We're told it's a national security secret. I began to perceive that our government was ruled increasingly by presidential directive; each president that came along began to increase the powers of the presidency. Nixon messed it up for a little while, but not a great deal. It's been going straight ahead ever since. It's been increasing with bounds ever since Nixon. And when I say presidential powers, it includes the bureaucracy, which in turn, I began to realize, was largely influenced by the defense manufacturing complex and the Department of Defense. These decisions are being made without any consultation at all. And nuclear threats have been made by every president since Truman, including Truman. Either implied or actual.

It's totally out of control. I don't think we have any control at all. They present a facade of cooperation with the people, but there is no consultation with them when they make these decisions, particularly in the realm of international policy and the development and use of atomic weaponry. There's no discussion with the electorate at all. They have nothing to say about it. They have allowed some protests, but if they get bad, you'll see what happens. If the protests get worse, I think we'd have a police state. We've almost got one now. We'll have a full police state. They'll come out in full panoply if the discussions and the objections get very forceful. You can see it rearing its ugly head in all directions. There's an attempt to muzzle the Supreme Court, there's an attempt to muzzle the media. There's more secret endeavors by the government, and they want even more. They want to be able to prevent any public access to government files of all kinds. More and more of them.

It'd be very easy to do it. All they've got to do is hold up the Russian bear high enough for everybody to get a good look at it, keep talking to it, and keep pointing at it. I'm surprised they haven't appointed the Big Dipper as the symbol. It's the constellation of the bear.

If we fall in this country, I think it'll be internally from destruction of our economic base, probably. If we should fall. And a great danger to the destruction of the economic base is the weapons race. It's, I think, the prime cause of our economic difficulties. It's true that the world started out with certain raw materials, and it's getting a little shorter on their reserves of fossil fuels, but if we didn't have this arms race on our hands, we could set our objectives and our endeavors, and end some of those problems rather quickly, I think. If we could get out from under control of this corporatocracy, which puts all sorts of impediments in the way of solving problems of energy and a lot of other problems that interfere with their manufacturing and distribution and profits at the present rate. Of course, there's money to be made in it, tremendous, big amounts of money, by the weapons manufacturers and their associated manufacturers. That particular thing permeates our whole country. Those manufacturing facilities are located in every state of the union. And nobody wants to put a stop to theirs because it would put too many people out of work.

A physician is trained to save lives, and when you see the world marching toward complete destruction you think you ought to at least make a statement on it. I joined that Physicians for Social Responsibility several years ago on that account, because I thought at least they were educating themselves. As a dues-paying member, I think I'm one of two in town, one of two doctors in a town of 150,000.

I talked to some, and they say, "Frank, we think you're right, but we've got patients out there at Pantex." A doctor's supposed to treat anybody, no matter what he believes or what he's done, but as for keeping their mouths shut, I don't see what that's got to do with it. It's because there's three thousand people and their families working out there. And there's a lot of influence out there. Pantex spends a lot of money. And they pay the highest salaries anywhere around here, much higher than construction work or commercial work or manufacturing.

I'm seventy-four years old. I've lived my life, and I've had a real nice one, a good one, an interesting one. Rewarding and challenging. I don't have a lot of fears for myself. My fears are for the world. We're heading right down the road to destroy everything on the face of the earth. And it's very anguishing to see it happening, and you wonder why people can't stop and see this. And put a stop to the policy decisions by their leaders who should know a lot better and should be making better decisions. I'm amazed, with the magnitude of the threat hanging over them, that people function as well as they do.

For years, I'd always felt that when I reached three-score years ten plus I could say what I thought as often as I wanted to say it. And that was one of the few compensations for reaching that exalted age. I always kind of thought that when you got there that people would listen to you, too. That they would give credit for your years of experience and your gray hairs. Instead of that, I've found that if you weren't real agile, you'd get slapped in the face with a dead fish for opening your mouth. That if you differed in opinion from the standardized opinions, that you would be divisive. If you proposed a new idea, that you would be seditious. And that if you promoted a new idea, you would be very apt to be accused of being a trai-tor. But in spite of that, I think this problem is sufficiently important to go right ahead and speak my piece about it. The difference between being a hero and a heretic is that the hero's idea prevails. That's the only differ-ence. Our founding fathers, if they hadn't prevailed, would have been a bunch of heretics and probably strung up by their necks.

Velia Garcia

One of the founders and organizers of Casa Amigo, a self-help community center in one of Albuquerque's Chicano neighborhoods, Velia Garcia traces her own heritage back through the Spanish to the native American. Casa Amigo is concerned with long-term issues such as land grant rights, water quality and the desecration of sacred burial grounds by uranium and coal mining. It is also vitally concerned with the day-to-day struggle for food and medical care for a people who are often passed over by the white culture.

22

Land grant is unique to New Mexico and southern Colorado. You don't find it anywhere else in the United States. It's similar to the native Americans. We're here forever. We come from the native Americans; my grandmother was Apache. When the Spanish colonized this area they used us as a buffer zone. They gave us large tracts of land, deeded to large families and held communally. This one was held by two hundred families, and it encompassed 82,000 acres. There are still 45,000 acres of communal lands intact in this grant.

There was a war between the United States and Mexico following the ouster of Spain, and a treaty followed which respected the rights of the people here. Up to twelve years ago, the land grants were still administered under a commission, the Land Grant Commission, by the heirs themselves. Then big corporations like Kerr-McGee Nuclear and Shell came in and convinced people to turn their grants into corporations. There was a lot of opposition. It was even illegal to do that according to the original treaty. They did it anyway, and now we're seeing big changes in terms of what happens here in the valley.

Out of three of the nation's weapons laboratories, we have two of them. We supply over 50 percent of the United States' uranium. And we're now slated to be the first dump for radioactive wastes. A complete cycle. The reason I think it's important to understand the history is because then we can understand how it is that they're able to do this to us. Because our way of life and traditions are very, very unique, these changes have created a lot of real divisions among the different people.

Often people who come here don't understand what it's like to be land based. There's a whole different set of values that comes from that. You have more respect for the land, more respect for the air, because you know you're going to be here forever. Like we don't plant until the moon's in a certain cycle, until the gravity is just right. We don't have operations in a full moon, and you don't travel then either. I see a big difference in those who are nomadic. We'll see people who live in New York and chase the money. When I'm in New York I get really like I can't conceptualize what people exist for. It's like they're just going to work and getting money, that's their whole way of life. Because how much can you make? And after a while you lose sight of your relationship to nature. You really lose sight, because there's not much nature in New York. Concrete and money. And for land-based people, materialism isn't the important thing—it's the people itself, and the land, and the ability to breathe right, to have good water and live a little bit longer.

There's been a recent immigration into our area from the East. And most people think that *we* immigrated. They think we've emigrated from Mexico. They really believe this. They really believe that my family was from Mexico City somewhere, and we came into the United States. But it was the other way around.

Look at the new people coming in and the way they relate to us. They still have the mentality that Polk had when he marched in—manifest destiny. The right to have the United States be from one border to the other, from sea to shining sea. This whole supremacy that is imprinted in people's heads still maintains here. For example, following becoming the state of New Mexico, we began to see a lot of the land being ripped off. We had an influx of lawyers from the East, challenging the people. Federal courts ruled on laws designed to take the land. And it's still happening today.

For example, the fifty wealthy families who control New Mexico are all white. All of them. In terms of economic power, we have no economic power. We have had political power recently in terms of Governor Anaya, but we have no base, no economic base. What we have is Robert O. Anderson, chairman of Atlantic Richfield Oil, who owns much of the land in New Mexico and who lives outside. He has his home base in Roswell, but he lives in California.

We have no industry. The largest employer is the federal government. We have a budget of $1.2 billion to run the state, and the federal government spends $1.9 billion. So the federal government subsidizes New Mexico, almost like what they do to some little island out in the Pacific. So the largest employer is the federal government, and the majority of that is all related to the military.

I have a friend, for example, who has his own little lathe set-up. He does piecework for Sandia Labs. And he's got another friend who does little screws or little parts for weapons. They have no idea it's weapons—what else does Sandia do? They're sitting there with all these pieces and have no idea what they're contributing to. And they're thankful to get that little piecework.

Look at what's happening with the United States in terms of the way the money's being used. The whole budget is geared toward the military and into developing arms. When you bring it down to New Mexico, it's worse here. We always hear about security – what does security mean? To me, when you talk about security, the furthest thing from my mind is a strong military. They talk about security and a strong nation. What do we want a strong nation for when our people are dying?

Right now, we have a food box, an emergency box. And it's really sad, because we get hit with more needs every day. People come here; they've lost their jobs, their social security's been taken away from them. Some have terminal cancer. Indiscriminately we got a call from the federal government – cut this many people off the rolls – and we have to do it. We get hit with increased needs, and they say, The people have to go and prove . . . go through a process, to prove they are ill. In the meantime, think of the mental health aspect of it. Somebody who's already dying is cut.

So our membership gets hit because we run the program on a volunteer basis. You have some little old lady sitting across from you who says they turned my gas off because I couldn't pay it. Where do you go to get help for her when there is no more help?

I remember the tenth grade here in Albuquerque, at the Valley High School. I joined the *Legend* staff, which is the school newspaper. They always used to rotate among us the responsibility of writing the editorial, so that we would get a flavor of all the facets of the way a newspaper was run. I wrote an editorial on conformity and nonconformity, and I'll never forget it. My sense was that when we're born they tell us that we have to be like a fish in a stream and swim with the current. And my question was, What if all the fish are swimming the wrong way? I think that we need some nonconformists so that we can start to make it better, or correct what's wrong. I gave some other examples of . . . I didn't feel I was born just to adapt there because I saw a lot of things that were not right, and I don't want to adapt to things that are wrong. I want to change it. So they refused to print my editorial. At that point, I didn't understand how to fight back. The way that I fought back is I got very angry with the school and I started to turn away. I wouldn't go to school. I was just pissed with them. And at that time there weren't many teachers who could relate to me. They tried to convince me that I was wrong, that I had to learn. My thinking was wrong; I had to learn to adapt because I was going to have a lot of problems. When I graduated, I got out of there with a 1.2. I barely got out, but they didn't kill my spirit.

I think what happens to a lot of us when we're in school – our creativity, our own initiative, is taken away. I do theater a little bit with my children. I have four kids, and so I try to incorporate them in what I do. I remember watching in the classroom when I go and help. They'll give all the kids a mimeograph art page. An apple with a leaf and a stem. Color number-two red, number-three is green, color number-three green. I said why don't you put the apple there and tell the kids, draw what *you* think the apple is like. And instead, they impose what they think are standardized concepts. And my thing is that each one of us is so unique, we have so much potential, such creativity, it would really help to make it a much better world if we were allowed to create, to develop the positive things that are inside of us.

Phillip Cassadore

Traditional Apache medicine man, i.e. spiritual leader, Phillip Cassadore carries with his person great centeredness, a certainty, or as the Japanese say, hara. *Any meeting scheduled with a traditional Indian spiritual is tenuous, as his order of things may change at the moment, depending upon the needs of his people. This basically different understanding of life, of the moment, is often in divergence with that perceived by whites, or "Europeans."*

23

A lot of Indians are faced with the problem of the materialism of the white society in conflict with their own background. They're confused, and it's awaiting them every time they leave the reservation, where they're with their own group, and go by their own way of life. Sometimes you experience it, especially like being a student, when you go into school.

The superintendent at San Carlos [Reservation] wanted to move all the Apache children into Globe High School so that the Indian kids could mingle with white kids and they could speak English faster, make good grades and then go higher, higher in society. I don't think the Indian went for that. They didn't. It doesn't mean anything to them . . . And they always wonder why Indians don't want to go to school. I think a lot of white kids don't like school, too. I'm saying that these Indians, when they go to school with white kids . . . there's no end to the confusion awaiting them. On their own, they were making good grades, and not competing with one another, beauty contests or sports. You play basketball not because you're going to be a champion basketball player. You play sports because it's just a sport. It's not to be one of the outstanding players in the world. That's the way they look at things, and I think that bothers them when they leave the reservation.

You might be an outstanding A-1 student all through high school and college, but you don't know anything. You just know everything by memorizing it. No understanding. That's not the way we teach our children. Mostly these are Europeans' ideas, nothing to do with being an Apache. It irritates me because I don't think they try to understand us, or accept our culture. They want our culture to be like theirs. Like if there were a bouquet of flowers, they want to say to the rose, why don't you be a daisy instead of a rose. They say the daisy is prettier. Europeans did this the world over.

I think a lot of white people don't know that their society is very highly competitive. Now we're having problems in the world. Which is the strongest? Which is the number-one nation? The United States or Russia?

There's a lot of problems on the reservation. Alcoholism is sky high; not only at San Carlos, all reservations have it. And they ask why, why do Indians drink too much? And then drugs. Drugs are a new thing, and Indians indulge in it, and they're just going crazy. And then Christians . . . I say they make you crazy. I don't want to apologize. I don't want to accommodate Christianity, to pave the way for it. All these Christians are making it worse. Now we have eighteen different denominations of churches at San Carlos, and everybody's just going crazy, like mentally insane.

Apache people in their normal way will speak slowly so that another person can hear the emotions they are saying with their words. Then this evangelist comes to San Carlos who was speaking so loud you couldn't sit as an Apache and hear what he was saying. I said that's angered spirit. They talked like they were very angry.

The white people divided the Apache into five different reservations. They also changed their names, and they also broke down their clan system. The Catholics came in and said you can marry your cousin, that's all right according to the Catholic religion. Protestant people came and told them to burn up all their history because that's the work of the devil. They said you're a reborn Christian, a born again Christian; you're going to live a new life. You just go to church, pray three times a day in church, and forget about making baskets. You cannot make baskets anymore or arts and crafts anymore. And then white people talk about why the Indians are not making arts and crafts anymore. Why did they forget how to make those? Now everybody's going crazy on the reservation, and they are wondering, "What's wrong with these Indians?"

Money talks in your society. You can do just anything – destroy the sacred mountains, everything, just for money. The way the Apache look at the land, it belongs to everybody. We're here to use this land. You can't put a fence around here and say this is my land. Europeans came here with the idea, this is mine. I bought it. I can put a fence around it.

White people can destroy the sacred mountains, the burial grounds, too, taking out coal and uranium. Indians know that taking out uranium, out of the ground, from their sacred land, will destroy the whole world. It came from their homeland, and then to make a nuclear bomb out of it will kill the whole of life on earth. Indians are very angry about this, and very sad.

At San Carlos we have a ceremonial for thirty days sometimes. We sing and dance and pray for thirty days. We think that it will change the attitude of people, and the world. We sing a snake song, sing a turtle song, sing a lizard song, sing a squirrel song, sing a song of anything that stings or has poisons, we have songs for that. Which I can't sing. I can't put that on my record and sell it because that's sacred. I can't do that. This is very different from European ways. And that's why the traditional ways are seen as a threat, because they're not tied into consumerism and materialism.

I own nothing myself. In my medicine bag I carry a few sacred things – bee pollen, eagle feather, etc. – but I try to understand the significance of all things. Birds, squirrels, snakes, all living things. Yesterday, I was lying in the dry wash, and a rattlesnake came by, and he's telling me to move because there's going to be a flash flood coming down pretty soon. It's like an instinct you already know. You're communicating with the snake. Some people don't understand this. But at San Carlos, the Apache don't get bit by rattlesnakes.

In the beginning, the Creator gave all the different races of people instructions on how to live. White people got the instructions; everybody got the instructions. Most people have forgotten the instructions. Traditional people still have their direct instructions. They consider everyone as an important person. Everybody – not just people with a Ph.D. degree. Everybody's considered as some worthwhile person to be on this earth.

Evarts Loomis

The founder and medical director of Friendly Hills Fellowship, a Quaker-inspired retreat and healing center in the high desert country of Southern California, Evarts Loomis is considered by many as the father of holistic medicine in the United States. A man of quick, seemingly boundless energy, Dr. Loomis's interest is the whole person: emotional, physical and spiritual. "We don't heal anybody. We're initiating a process within."

24

As a college student I went to a Quaker school. Actually, I didn't know anything about Quakerism before that, but I soon learned about the American Friends Service Committee and realized, Here's a group that is really not just talking about peace, they're doing something about it. Their motive is not money, certainly. In fact, the average Quaker worker doesn't get more than a few dollars a month. When I worked with the American Friends Service Committee during the Second World War I was getting ten dollars a month. Dealing with small sums, we know it doesn't go into a lot of red tape.

I was a physician. And just the Quaker idea that we have a wisdom within ourselves that's really our contact with God and our interrelatedness appealed to me very strongly. We are all part of a great system of energies, call it whatever we want. I've observed so much in sickness that the sick person is a separated person. And of course, war just produces separation. It doesn't bring people together. It just makes more animosity. Somebody hurts somebody in a war, therefore they have to come back and do it to somebody else. It's an endless thing, and has been going on for centuries. It's about time we grew up and realized we've got to get out of the child-hood stage and start to meet with love.

The sick person is the separated person, and when they begin to get well, they lose this sense of separation. It doesn't make any difference what the illness is, it applies I believe to all types of illness. That as they get better, there begins to be a sparkle in their eyes, they begin to find that they can relate to others much better.

I'm seventy-five years old now. It was the Germans when I started, First World War. And then it was the Italians, Mussolini. And then it was the Spanish under Franco. And then it was the Japanese, and then it's the Russians, the Chinese. In other words, these people *out there* are scapegoats.

Sometime we're going to have to be adult enough to realize that the problem out there is not the communists or the Russians, it's the war within me. I can't face my own problems in life, so I have to project them to somebody else, and eventually on a societal level we're doing it to whole nations. Because we're not strong enough to see our own problems.

As Norman Cousins says, legalized insanity is now going on, manufacturing nuclear bombs and that type of thing. We're told that nuclear power is essential because oil's giving out. We haven't even looked at solar energy. The problem with solar energy is you can't harness money to it; it's free. I think that's the big catch. I think the danger today is that our greed is catching up to us. We've got to learn that we are our brother's keeper, that we're all interrelated. We're all a part of each other. We can't be prepared to kill somebody else and find peace within ourselves; it's impossible. If I hurt somebody else, it's going to bounce right back on me.

Perhaps the most remarkable person I've met that's really interested in peace is a person most people have never heard of. His name is Robert Muller. He's the assistant secretary general of the UN, been there for thirty-three years. Probably knows the world better than anybody else living today – a person on a real spiritual search. He coordinates the thirty-two organizations of the UN and has written a book called *Most of All, They Taught Me Happiness*. In this book, he describes working with U Thant, who was his great spiritual teacher, and with Dag Hammarskjöld, and the impression these men made on him. The sad thing to him is why the news media won't pick up what the UN is doing. The UN is doing tremendous things. Many of the African conflicts that could have resulted in wars as new nations were born were settled in the UN.

To me, it's so much more exciting working toward health, which you can connote with peace in the human mind, rather than working with disease. How I happened to think of Muller was Muller says, "I'm not interested in people that are fighting war. I'm working for pro-peace." He says, "The rest of my life is going to be spent in working toward peace. Because that which we fight is likely to get us sooner or later." Jesus made a very important statement when he said, "Resist not evil, but overcome evil with good." Because resistance sets up disease. And so I think we really need to get to this movement of pro-peace. As an individual person, I must find my own peace of mind. If I sufficiently radiate peace, others will be attracted to me, be interested in what I'm doing.

Melinda Rector

On her way to the Women's Peace Encampment in Seneca Falls, New York, Melinda (here on the left) and her children were visiting with friends in Berkeley when I met them. Santa Cruz is her home community.

25

I have this feeling that we don't even know the all of what we're doing. It's very exciting. There's six of us, and then we all have friends who have friends, so it's more than just us – this feeling that something is coming through us, and we're being used in a new way, or very old way, where we're combining politics and "culture-carving." That's what a friend of mine calls it. We're learning new ways to support each other as family members. We're learning to help each other during births and after births with meals and support. We help each other in our marriages; we help each other with child-raising. So it was natural for peace issues to come up.

One of us last year said, "I would love to go to that disarmament rally, but we can't go because we're nursing. Maybe we could send Dale, that's my husband, because he speaks four languages." And this other daddy is a photographer, how perfect. The exciting thing was that we weren't anybody in particular. We didn't have to join a group. We were just neighbors, anybody down the street. We made our own group. In two weeks we raised a thousand dollars to send them.

When they came back from the rally, we transcribed the tapes and did a presentation in church and invited a lot of people. They had also taken letters with them from families we knew. Letters, pictures, drawings that their children had done. Dale got them out to different people from all over the world: some were distributed to a couple from El Salvador, some to somebody from Canada living in a commune, some to folks from England. That's what I want to do, too, going back to Seneca Falls. That way you take the spirit and energy from people back with you.

The Greenham Commons women in England have been magical. There's a picture of them dancing on a missile silo. You can't dance on a missile silo. That's incredible. And playing snakes under these long blankets. Getting into the base under these blankets and making soldiers run out and try to catch them. You just can't be a soldier and be running around catching people. It breaks that spell. And that's exciting. I'm hoping to take part in some very unexpected things myself.

They get arrested, get thrown in jail. One woman who was thrown in jail turned her sentence into a fund-raiser, a "jailathon." People sent her money for every day she was in jail. It's like Aikido, where you take that energy that may be negatively directed at you, and you turn it to your own good. You use that energy. That's the idea. If you're thrown in jail, then you don't let that be *their* experience; it's *yours*.

I used to be an activist when I was a teenager. I went to a few army depot bases myself, and I went down to Mississippi. Then a little bit later on, I realized that I was yelling for peace, and I was full of hostility. So I did a real about-face, and I went on a mystical path, which I'm still on, the path of meditation. For fifteen years I hadn't done anything like this, but something clicked last summer, where now my meditation continues out to the world. So, rather than a split between my inner and my outer, this is a connection, my duty as a citizen.

We're citizens of this planet. We all need to take a piece of that responsibility. I spend most of my time taking care of my kids, but just as a citizen of the world, I can take off a little bit of time for the planet, for the good. I'd rather be gardening, much rather be down with my basil patch, but this is my duty. Wanting to be alive now.

Dale and I talk about the connection between Sears and what's happening in El Salvador. The connection between somebody's microwave oven and people being oppressed in these different countries. We've made a personal commitment to being poor – by default. It feels appropriate to be thinking of less economically all the time.

Take something like the way land is used. Big companies invest in Third World countries where they raise a product that is a luxury for us, that people in their own country can't afford, say coffee. We can buy it, we can afford it, so the people in that country – if they owned their own land, they could be growing enough food to feed themselves and their families – grow coffee for us, which they can't afford for themselves. They are at the poverty level. It rapes in many ways. If one crop is grown massively, acres and acres of coffee, that's going to effect the ecological balance as well. You get more bugs. Then you've got to spray, and so we sell them pesticides. The pickers inhale that, I get it in my coffee or in my bananas, they get it in their lungs, and the earth becomes more destroyed. And the product costs more because it's on TV. You can sort of jump on at any level and it draws the same picture. How does this go with the arms race? You need arms to keep the people down who aren't satisfied about their situation.

I think at this point it's time to stand up, for women and their men friends to stand up. I'm excited about women's energy right now, very excited.

As women, I see that we have had the source of our power disguised and cut off from us for many hundreds of years. Now it's coming to the surface. Women are reclaiming their mythological roots as storers of life. Women's songs, women's history, more women archaeologists uncovering things. We're reclaiming this, and we're seeing that it's not to be more like men, but it's incredible, those ovaries are incredible. They are the source of life, and we know that. We've got to remember it. And use that.

Anybody who's had a baby . . . you can't hold a baby in your arms and not take some risks for preserving the future. There's this incredible schizophrenic existence we have to live under now. I'm nursing my baby, and on the other hand, the kids are talking about the future, and I can't tell them there's going to be one. Yet I can't spread my despair to them; on one hand it's talking positively, and on the other hand there's this wound that just keeps stabbing—that actual physical threat that we may blow ourselves up. I can't forget that. We spend a lot of our time covering that up.

I can't help but think that some people have lost a lot of their will to live, their vision about the world being good. That the world's kind of crummy and, in a way, dying would be a wonderful escape from all this tension and madness. People who live in a rat-race world must feel that a lot. Not consciously, I think.

In our baby group, Families for Peace, we notice that at different times one or the other of us will drop the ball. We're supposed to be working on a project, and somebody isn't getting that meeting happening. They have frozen up, and we have to dethaw them. We have to keep working on staying with this. It's scary and awful. We're finding that it's too scary to deal with alone. But if you are working with other people you can deal with it. If you keep it alive and keep it moving it seems to make all the difference. It's too much for anybody to feel on their shoulders.

My hope is somehow that people who are in decision-making positions will get thawed out. I read something very inspiring recently. Maureen Dean said if she'd known about Watergate and if Pat Nixon had known about it, it wouldn't have happened. If the wives had said, that's a rotten idea, Dick. All the wives everywhere, that's a lot.

In Santa Cruz with my community, we dance a lot. We've been studying African dancing. We bring our children and they dance. African dancing is like the heartbeat of the earth. It's sexy, but in a real positive way, not in a covert way, in a very up-front way. Dancing is my favorite thing to do, the most fun. We're learning to drum. There are drummers who come from Oakland and San Francisco and local drummers. Black and white. Somehow we white people need to learn this from Africans. They have a lot to offer us.

We don't want to live abstractly. We're really dancing with each other. We're really helping each other give birth to our children. We're really taking a meal if a woman is bleeding or sick or if a man has lost his job. We'll really loan him the money or give it to them. We're really helping. It's simple. It doesn't sound like anything when I say it, but I know I've come a long way from being that one step removed. The way I grew up, everybody lived in their own little box.

There's so much trouble now, people have lost so much faith, and a good deal of it stems from having to be so faceless. If we could be more accountable to one another, lived in smaller units, larger than a nuclear family but smaller than just being an anybody on the block, it seems like that just takes care of so much that's wrong. Old people are taken care of in that way, children are taken care of. People do group gardens, group fun. A lot of it, in my thinking, hearkens back to that. The way Indians lived in California before we all moved in.

I think that it behooves us to be very creative in our politics at this point. We have nothing to lose. Frances Moore Lappe said we need to risk being wrong and making mistakes. We can always find out the proper quote or the right answer later. But to risk, that's what's exciting.

Alia Johnson

In their desire to find "a better game than war," Alia Johnson and her husband, Bob Fuller, have developed an ongoing group process named for the fifth-century-B.C. Chinese diplomat and peacemaker, Mo Tzu. Among the places they and their small band of travelers have been are Vietnam, Russia, Ireland, Israel, Poland and Kenya. As non-partisan individuals, they attempt to go into another culture with a willingness to see one's own culture and a rival one as complementary, which involves a radical shift away from dualistic, possessive presuppositions to a more inclusive world view. Alia and Bob live in Berkeley with their young sons, Adam and Noah.

26

We call it a project, but even that's getting shaky. One of the last words we had for it was a colloquium. Mo Tzu is really a loose-knit network of people who travel. We travel a lot, and we think about questions of war and peace from a perspective that tries to transcend political partisanship. Bob's definition, which he likes to say, is finding what you love and what you hate. Which has some validity in my experience. When you actually go on a trip, if you're a normal human being who is honest about your emotions, you really see a lot of what you hate. For a long time, on these trips, I went through tremendous emotional turmoil. It was awful.

In Russia, in Ireland. It happens everywhere. I go so deeply into the feelings of everybody in the country, so I'm basically walking around in hatred. And living with it in a very present way. It's right there in your own body. I try to process everything through myself.

In Israel, we were living with the Jews, and hearing the stories of the Holocaust and hearing the rationalizations of their behavior. At that time they were preparing to invade Lebanon and being particlarly violent in their own behavior. In the midst of this, I started visiting the Palestinians and seeing people, kids, who had just come out of jail after being tortured for five days straight by Israelis. Saw soldiers shooting at little girls in Bethlehem. Little girls who were stoning them. Stuff like that. It makes you hate them all. It's really bad. So you just keep going and exposing yourself and talking to a lot of people on a really deep level until you begin to understand what their real story is. That's coming to compassion the hard way. You think you arrive with it, then you lose it. For me, the only way to really process something is to really get into it. At least that's the only way I've ever found.

Jerusalem's full of guns. It took me weeks just to get used to that. I remember precisely when the full feeling changed. I was in Jerusalem, getting on a bus, and there was a little old lady, eighty years old, sitting on the bus. In came this beautiful young Jewish guy, carrying this gun, and sat down beside her. I thought, Oh, that's why that gun is there. It's because she went through the Holocaust, and she wants this young man to guard her. Just like oh, of course, he should be there. Suddenly, I accepted that that's how it is. Any moralizing about it is really irrelevant. It happens time and time again, going into the horribleness of it all and finally coming to an understanding.

We project our shadow onto others. In Ireland, the Protestants project their shadow on the Catholics. And vice versa. No question about it. It's all very explicit and down in writing. The main characteristics seem to be that the bad guy is more of an underdog, is often more poor, and less "civilized" by your own standards. It was true in Africa. All of Africa was colonized because Europe projected its shadow. They went in and said we're going to fix this. Get some clothes on, stop screwing around. They did that to an entire continent. That's what we'd do to Russia if we could.

How to withdraw those projections? I don't know. I just stopped hating my husband this year. I bought him this postcard the other day that said we went through a lot together, and most of it was your fault. I didn't hate him any more than everybody else hates their husband. One of the things we use a lot, both in our work and in our own family peacemaking, is humor. Really exaggerating everything and making it up so that it's so disgusting you have to laugh at it. It really helps. Occasionally you get a shoe thrown back at you, but it keeps moving the unconscious to the conscious.

It's a strange thing, but I'm not that interested in peace. My interest really is in truth. It's true that understanding cures. Understanding the process that the culture's going through now, that the world is going through now. Understanding what our job is in this world right now. What it is we're supposed to be doing, what it is we can be doing. What our opportunity is. For me, the nuclear war issue is like a gigantic spotlight that makes everything more vivid, everything more real, everything more urgent.

One of the reasons why I'm not interested in peace is because the way people think about peace doesn't usually take into consideration the passion and aggression which people have that's really positive. Noah came in the other day and said, "Mom, would you please kill Adam?" Adam came running in to tell me his side. And I said, "Adam, will you get me a big knife out of the kitchen? Noah's just asked me to kill you. I'm going to give in to this." And they both looked at me like, oh, I really don't mean it.

I asked myself for a long time, Why are all those generals out there? Why are these guys flying around over my head with bombs in their bellies? What have I to do with that? I was standing in my kitchen asking myself that question for the thousandth time, kind of absent-mindedly staring at my refrigerator. Then it struck me, they're guarding my refrigerator. They're there because I want to be rich. I've got the Berkeley Police, the State National Guard, the entire United States Army guarding the quiche Lorraine in my refrigerator so that the poor people in Oakland, in Guatemala and all the other people will not only refrain from eating my quiche Lorraine but will continue working for thirty cents an hour to fill my refrigerator, etc., etc. That is the fact of my life. There is no way to get around it; that's the reason they're there.

It's just part of the whole structure of the world economic system now that we have to have nuclear weapons. It's part of this particular game. I want to be rich and powerful. Now the question is, Why am I so attached to being rich? I think it goes back to the basic first denial of death in life. I think that if I'm rich I won't die, at a simple psychological level.

I don't have to worry about material things. I'm not living on the edge. My children are in no danger of being hungry. I sit in Berkeley cafes and drink my cappuccino and all's right with the world. We live on the edge relative to most people of our age and talent in upper middle class America, but we're also fabulously rich compared with anybody else in the world.

You know how I felt when we went to Kenya? We would go through these villages with the very, very poor people, and I had the strangest emotional reaction. I decided I wanted to live in the Waldorf Astoria on strawberries and cream and go to the opera. I have never had such a desire in my entire life. But that was my reaction to being in Kenya. I wanted to get as far away as possible from confronting what I was confronting. I wanted to move into the Hilton in the air conditioning. It was very interesting to see these desires that went through my body.

One of the great values of Mo Tzu work is simply taking responsibility without guilt for who you are, who your country is, the fact that you're an American and what you're doing. And I swear, I learned to do it. I'd go in there and I would say, Here we are. I'd talk to people. One of the things you learn very quick is, don't apologize. You don't rationalize; you don't say, "Aren't Americans terrible for doing this." If you say that you're just playing the game, you're just continuing the war. So you come in naked with respect to positions. You don't say, "Oh, isn't it terrible that I bought the guns that beat you over the head. And I'm terribly sorry." You don't say, "Well, I can't help it, it's Ronald Reagan's fault and I'm here to fight against Ronald Reagan."

To just go in and process it without any padding of any kind of ideology is really such an incredible practice. You find that in Mo Tzu work that it's really the only thing worth doing without interpretation. And it's amazing what happens when you do that. It's so awkward and so painful you think you're going to die. To just sit there and see the other person saying, "Well, there's a rich American lady – *da di da di da* – and she must think this . . ."

And I'm sitting and thinking, This person must hate me because . . . You have to go through all that. What it teaches you is to hold responsibility for who you are and what your country is in a way you usually don't have the opportunity to do. Usually we just stand around having opinions.

The privilege that I feel when I visit anywhere else in the world, including Europe, is not my material wealth and not even my political freedom, although it's related to that. It's the freedom of mind. It's like I am capable of sustaining and understanding five different ideologies, five different religious beliefs and how they relate to each other. I'm not attached to my culture in certain ways. I'm not enslaved by it. Because of my education, because of my political freedom. That's the thing about being an American that feels like a real privilege.

It's a complete mystery to me that we are not communicating with understanding of having anything to do with the military. The whole peace movement is still . . . 90 percent of us are pointing our finger saying, you're the bad guys, we're the good guy. That's horseshit.

Helen Caldicott believes that the American generals are totally evil. She recently described them as less than human. This is not a good start. I have written some communications which I haven't figured out what to do with yet, that have to do with acknowledging to the military that they are doing the best they know how, given their assumptions, to prevent war. That's what they're doing. In fact the guys up there, flying around over our heads now, are being very careful not to drop the bomb on us. He's sober, he's learned to fly his plane real well, and he's doing a job that is very hard and has tremendous responsibility, tremendous moral stuff. No one's supporting him. I don't know how to do it, but somehow we've got to figure out how to communicate with them in a healing way.

One way I have hope is simply to give up blaming and accept joyfully the burden, the opportunity or the burden, that's given to us. And for that we have to grow up. One of the people in my Women, War and Peace group was absolutely shocked to hear that I don't hate Ronald Reagan. She said, "What do you mean you don't hate Ronald Reagan; I get up every morning and I hate him. That's what I have for breakfast." For me, it is a tremendous personal liberation to have stopped hating Ronald Reagan.

I'm angry at Ronald Reagan for exactly the same reasons that I'm angry at my two-year-old spilling milk. I want him to be somebody else; I want him to be grown-up, to take care of this little problem of nuclear war so that I can go around and do whatever I do. But it's childish to be angry with him. He's my president; he works for me; I pay his salary. I have had an opportunity to grow up in a different way than he has, and it's my responsibility to handle my life in as powerful a way as I can. Once you get off blaming, your freedom increases enormously.

It's a strange, strange time to live in. We're confronting something, and I think part of the pain and part of the difficulty that the world is having is that suddenly we have to hold so much more information and so much more responsibility than anyone in the world has ever had to before. We have to know about the starving children in Biafra; we have to know about nuclear weapons; we have to know about the people in Oakland who are starving; and we have to know about ourselves. We no longer believe that we're innocent; we're no longer identified with our superegos, to put it briefly. We have to know about what's inside of us; we have to know about everything that's going on in the world. War is just one part of that.

Kit Bricca and Joy Marcus

Kit Bricca and Joy Marcus are a husband and wife team who founded "a center to prevent nuclear annihilation" in the former garage of their rented home in El Granada, California, a tiny (population 2,800) fishing community about thirty-five miles south of San Francisco. The "center to prevent nuclear annihilation" conducts programs and workshops primarily focused on challenging the individual to make significant changes in his or her life. It is also a place of celebration. Kit and Joy are high energy individuals, as is their daughter, Laura, age five. Joy came to this out of her work in the Radical Psychiatry Movement in Berkeley; Kit has long been a political organizer and is also a counselor—working especially with violence in men.

27

Joy: In 1976 I started noticing that clients of mine were depressed in a way that seemed more massive than the usual sort. It went beyond needing love and work, something bigger than that. At the same time, I began to become more aware of items in the newspaper that referred to nuclear weapons buildup, and I realized that I'd been getting this information for a while and I had been screening it out. It began to occur to me that there was a connection between the massive depression that I was seeing in my clients and the information they were receiving about the world and denying or screening out.

I started to ask my clients if they ever thought about nuclear war. It was amazing what I observed. People were relieved to be asked that question. Some people said, "No, no, I never think about it, " but most people who were asked the question would have something to report. It was a subject that had been for a long time taboo.

Kit: As an organizer, I've had the privilege of working together with small groups of people that have made substantial social change. I happened to become a draft resister and be in touch with draft resisters at a time when the notion of somebody turning their draft card in and resisting the government of the United States was not common. My own decision to do it was based upon – I had no children at the time – the image of my twelve-year-old son asking me, "Papa, where were you during Vietnam?" That's what I had to live up to. It's the kind of person I wanted to be, and particularly the kind of man I wanted to be. Because this draft card was a rite of passage, an initiation into what it meant to be a man in United States society.

While I was waiting for my trial, I went to work in the United Farm Workers Union and saw incredible changes being made by a relatively few dedicated people. Then I met a woman whose parents were killed in World War II as a result of Nazis and who knew something about Amnesty International, which basically didn't exist in the United States in 1973. I went to work with her, and a small group of us put Amnesty on the map in this country. So I'd had the experience that it's possible for people to make change, and to really affect public opinion.

Part of the perspective that I see is there's a real collusion of all our consciousness on the history of war and the inevitability of war. People don't talk about there always seems to be peace going on. It's always like there always seems to be a war going on somewhere. And if you look, I think, at the bulk of people's lives, there is an enormous striving in people throughout the world to do what they've got to do to feed, clothe, shelter – to take care of themselves. And to go about it in a fairly direct way. We don't give ourselves enough credit for the things that actually bring security.

I think one of the things that is most important for security is that people learn how to cooperate with each other to get what they need. The phenomenon of war is glamorous in large part because here's an emergency, people have to cooperate. The excuse is you get to go fight a battle. Gandhi always talked about, what is it that . . . until there's enough commitment for people to gather together in a crisis situation and be willing to be killed as a nonviolent army, until that has enough mass appeal we won't see the changes needed.

I think the large appeal of war and armies is that people are going to learn some skills of cooperation. They're going to be thrust together, black and white; they're all going to be equal; they're going to have the same jobs – this kind of phenomenon. I think it's an organizational task, and I think what we're going to see in the next ten to twenty years are small-scale, internationally organized nonviolent armies. People that are just going to take it on, and they're going to go into conflict situations and risk being killed for a reason.

Joy: The reality is that it's too expensive to have a nuclear arms race. If a bomb is never dropped, we're being killed daily, slowly starved. We're being morally and spiritually starved, and destroyed as a society. The majority of people in the United States are suffering unconscionably because of the arms race. Psychologically, socially, economically and spiritually. There are people growing up feeling that they have no future. I happen to feel I have a future because I'm going to do everything I can to make sure I have one. I can't say if we're going to prevent nuclear war. I think we have as good a chance of preventing it as not.

Kit: If you took an unemployment line that is created by the present military budget – meaning the jobs that are lost due to the choices of going for the building of missiles, etc. – and line those people up, arm on shoulder, it would start in New York, and you know how far the line would go? All the way. Right through to the Pacific Ocean.

Joy: One of the underpinnings of the society is violence, mostly against women and children. That's a fear that I as a woman and a mother live with constantly. My hope is that by addressing the problem of the possibility of nuclear war, people will also begin addressing the reality of violence in daily life. And simultaneously work to prevent both. I don't think people would consider violence an option for the solution of conflict if war wasn't considered an option in our society. If war were totally abolished as an option, I think people would begin rethinking how they use violence to resolve conflict. And vice versa. They are very related.

Kit: Most of my work in the last year has been with men who are batterers, men who beat up women. I'm a consultant with a women's shelter here and the coordinator of a men's program in Marin County which has a hot line and drop-in groups and long-term groups. We have a place where men can come. The number-one violent crime in the country is domestic violence, according to FBI statistics, and it's the most highly underreported crime. I think the term domestic violence is a misnomer, a euphemism. In most cases we're talking about violence by men against women and children – 90-some percent.

Imagine if two or more men in a given neighborhood, an apartment house, condominium, workplace, got together and said, "OK, we're going to make it *our* business when we hear about a guy beating up his woman friend or his wife or the kids. This is *our* business. This is *our* neighborhood, this is *our* workplace." If they would on their own go to him, sit down together and say, "We know what's happening and we want you to know that we're here to help you. We're men too, we understand this, we understand. We're here to help you. We don't want this. This doesn't go in our neighborhood. Since we know about it, we're accomplice to a criminal activity. It's against the law to hit your wife."

Talk about battering as a moral issue, *talk* about battering as a legal issue, *talk* about battering as a work-related issue. Have different organizations working at it, each as their problem. At the same time have overall community education through mass media, and it's going to happen. And at the same time have direct service components, numbers where people can call, can get help, and that becomes widely known, then I think we're going to see some changes. If it becomes embarrassing, really embarrassing or shameful to hit your wife, to go to war, then we're really going to really see the potential for some larger-scale conversions.

The way between here and a violence-free society is that we create models. If a group of people can say this is *our* problem and we're going to take care of it. This is a community problem – it's not a family problem, it's not a personal problem, it's a community problem. We all share responsibility. Then we can do it in a geographic area, and the next step will be the declaration of the city mothers and fathers of a town to say, "We declare this area a battering-free zone, a violence-free zone." Can you imagine?

Nuclear-free zones. Which is a strategy of European communities and Third World communities. We're going to get these out of here. We're not going to attack you, and we don't want to be attacked, so we don't want them here.

The very skills that are learned on a small-scale community basis with interrupting sexism and violence are the very same skills and consciousness needed on the international level. What better way to train people in international diplomacy than to start right here, at home.

Joy: I think cooperation is fun. I think resolving conflicts cooperatively is a lot more fun than beating people up. I've been in the movement a long time, and I've always insisted that I enjoy myself. And I've always insisted that the people who work with me figure out what's fun for them to do, and do it. That's how work gets done. People do what really turns them on. This is not to say that we don't all have to share the work and take out the garbage. We all need to share that; it's just to say that I have enormous faith in people's capacity to know how to unite in work that needs to be done, that's exciting and delightful.

Kit: We visited with a very good friend from New York, Stan, and Laura was being very insistent. We were in the middle of talking. She's going, "Mama, Papa. Mama, Papa. I want the baby, the *baby*; I *want* the baby." And Stan and I looked at each other and came out with it at the same time. Can you imagine the people of the world with that amount of insistence, that amount of energy, that amount of humor, that amount of dogged determination saying "Dismantle the bombs"? Now. Dismantle the bombs. Dismantle the bombs. We're not leaving until you dismantle the bombs. Whenever I start to lose it and get serious, I just think of Laura. God, this is how to go about life.

Ada Sanchez

In the course of discovering her true heritage, Ada Sanchez (second from left) has come to realize deep understanding of herself, her heritage and the world. Now living in Milwaukie, a suburb of Portland, Oregon, she is an especially delightful and wise young woman.

28

My college training was in social work, and I worked with emotionally and physically battered children in a Puerto Rican neighborhood in Philadelphia, and at St. Christopher's Hospital for Children, in the child psychiatry center. I began to see a lot of connections between the economic situation the parents found themselves in and how they took it out on someone less powerful than they were, the husband taking it out on his wife or children.

Police brutality was real intense under Rizzo, and kids would come in traumatized from seeing their uncle or somebody beaten up, or being beaten themselves. The Ph.D.s and the psychiatrists in the center would not deal with any of the political connections.

The clincher came when a man was beaten to death in front of his home, and his nine-year-old daughter was brought in; I saw everybody when they first came in, because I was the intake caseworker on duty. There was an instantaneous candlelight vigil in the community that night, and hundreds and hundreds of people were out on the streets. The next day there were cops everywhere. I counted sixty-three in a one-block radius. They set up tents in Huntington Park; they were on buses, on horses, everywhere.

The people in the community decided to have a candlelight vigil until they could get Rizzo to come out and publicly say he'd do something about the police brutality. This was the first thing I ever helped organize, a march on City Hall. Rizzo came out and said it didn't mean anything because he knew what was going on all along.

These frustrations kept building up, especially when the Ph.D. types and the psychiatrists would not become a part of the organizing around going to City Hall. "I'm a professional, leave that up to those people." They weren't even being honest about what was really going on, in reports or records. So I just felt more and more like I was applying band-aids to systemic problems, and that the priorities in our society were leading to the situation were promoting the racist policies of that police department.

I began realizing the connection between a militaristic way of relation to the world, which filtered all the way down to how police related to people on the street, and how the guy related to his wife and kids. None of that was going to change until some basic priorities changed, because all the way down the line people felt justified in mimicking a very power-mongering militaristic controlling sort of attitude. Beginning with our leaders, whom people emulated the most.

At the same time this was happening, I was looking for other models around the globe or within this country that promoted other ways of relating to nature, the world and each other. The closest I could find were the American Indians.

I did not understand at first why I felt such a compulsion towards the Indians in this country. It wasn't until years later that I realized that was my own heritage. It was such a delight to begin unfolding my own true heritage, for a personal experience I could carry into political understanding.

Gradually I came to understand that even though my language heritage is Spanish, that was not my real culture. They were the conquistadors, the conquerers of another age. They put an artificial society into that which already existed. I came to discover a whole Indian nation called the Arawak, who lived along the Lesser Antilles in the West Indies and in Puerto Rico, or Borinquen, as its natural name was before the Spanish. For the most part they were a very peaceful society whose spiritual symbol of a circle with two faces on either side represented woman and man, as totally equal.

I found that for Indians the whole idea of consensus, coming to a common agreement or way of proceeding on a problem, is very significant. A number of peace groups and women's groups use that process; Quakers have a history of it. The basic underlying motivation is an understanding that each of us as individuals need to empower ourselves, need to feel the strength and the beauty of our individual energies and who we are as individuals. Our visions of what we would like in this world are just as real as the visions of the militarists, the racists or whoever. We are only limited by our faith or our belief in those visions.

As a group, then, if you combine your visions, you really intensify your ability to make that vision real, because you project a mental picture of what is possible. Anything you create, you have to think of it first. Then that vision becomes translatable.

What was valuable to me in the American Indian experience was learning practical ways to empower yourself. Seeing yourself as an individual whose mental and physical energy mattered, made a difference, was part of the whole.

Indians don't turn their power over to anyone. They know the power resides within, and it resides within all of us. You don't turn the power over to the big chief in the White House; you don't turn the power over to the big chief in the sky. The power is in all of us, is all of us.

Empowerment is part of that whole process of learning to use imagination again. If you go into a sweat – for instance, it's still dark, four o'clock in the morning or so, and you don't come out again until it's light. It's a sort of birthing experience. Once you have grounded yourself – that whole feeling as though you were a tree, connected to your roots and your branches – all these possibilities reach out. You feel centered yourself, and at the same time connected with others. There's almost a tangible inner circle of energy; it's new birth. What you choose to do with it depends upon where your heart is.

To know that right off we're in the spirit of nonviolence when dealing with a detrimental industry such as nuclear power plants or something, and realizing that we as individuals have power to resist that, to not cooperate, to interfere in some way. Not in a negative sense, but that if you interfere and stop it, then you have the opportunity, and responsibility, to turn it around and create something else. You don't just stop.

Indian cultures offer us a lot as to how we can cooperate better with each other, how we can deal with some of the ownership feelings and acquisitiveness that I think are the underpinnings of why certain people are trying to protect what they have acquired with something as exaggerated as nuclear weapons. Many people are suffering because a few are maintaining privileged status in society and in the world.

Our society doesn't want us to empower ourselves. It's specifically designed that way. In school, we are not taught that our opinion matters, that we can make a difference, that we are unique, that we have something to contribute. School weans that out of you. Most religions wean that out of you; your family for the most part weans that out of you; and then of course you're being prepared for work in some factory where you're not supposed to care what the product results in. You're supposed to care about your paycheck at the end of the week and to repeat that whole cycle again of putting it back into the nuclear family, sending your kids to school, etc., etc. This maintains a system in which decisions are made by a select few, which keeps power in the hands of the rich and those making huge profits off of weapons. The market for plutonium, for example, is more lucrative than heroin.

To me, a militaristic mindset takes out of our control our basic ability to live on this planet and pretty much control our lives, make decisions. Since we don't have that, we're in the process of having to grab it back. Once we grab it back, we can become the authors of that new life, that new birth-right, and the new understanding of it. Usually it's passed on from genera-tion to generation and you sort of accept it. These whole issues bring into question every aspect of our lives; how we relate sexually, how we relate in families, how we relate in schools, in religion, so on and so forth. If we weren't so threatened that all these things could be destroyed, we possibly wouldn't also be in a position where we could be looking completely anew, completely fresh, as though the whole world had been destroyed and started all over again.

There is great joy in being able to reclaim our birthright and being able to define it. If we can face that which we fear the most, and walk into it, we can turn it into an opportunity. The potential is just amazing. It's basically turning around.

If I can get over my fear – looking down at the ground a lot and not meeting people's eyes – if I can get up and speak in front of large audiences and that sort of thing, anybody can. My own personal evolution of con-sciousness is my biggest hope. I'm no different than anybody else.

Jim Douglass

Besides the huge U.S. Naval Trident Submarine Base, all that remains of the town of Bangor, Washington, is the old stationmaster's house, on a little hill a few feet above the railroad tracks, less than fifty yards from the railroad entrance to the giant facility. In the old stationmaster's house live Jim and Shelly Douglass, their two sons and assorted pets. It is from here that the Douglasses monitor the "Death Trains" or "White Trains" that arrive about twice weekly with a fresh cargo of hydrogen warheads. Long known as a writer and activist in theological and peace questions, Jim is now also recognized as a "train buff."

29

Ground Zero was created out of the context of the Trident Campaign, which began as an experiment in Gandhian nonviolence by a group of people who believed and continue to believe in nonviolence as a way of life. As an experiment in the power of nonviolence we began a campaign to explore that power and to, in the course of it, try to stop a submarine and missile system that we had been informed of by its designer, Robert Aldridge.

He had been working sixteen years for Lockheed Missiles and Space Corporation and had designed Polaris, Poseidon and Trident missile systems. In the course of designing Trident, he became aware of its purpose as a first-strike weapon and could not in conscience continue doing that, and in January 1973 he resigned from Lockheed.

He and Janet were both forty-seven when he resigned, and they had ten children. They had to change their whole way of life, and that moved us to a response. We began working on this campaign in January 1975. By 1977 we felt it was an act of violence to come in to the area, hold demonstrations and then retreat to our own residences rather than sharing the situation here with people who are dependent on Trident economically and through social and political pressures. So we decided to try to establish a center for nonviolence near the Trident base.

We felt that just coming in and holding a demonstration is a form of violence itself, in the sense of our attitudes towards people and the assumptions that we brought into those actions without sharing the situation, which is quite pressurized here in Kitsat County where people either work for Trident Base, the Puget Sound Naval Shipyard, or the Keyport Torpedo Station, which are all nuclear-related naval installations. And if they don't work for one of those three, they're liable to have a service station or something that's dependent on that. The entire county is dependent on the U.S. Navy for its economy.

We began holding these weekly meetings at Ground Zero, and we began to leaflet the workers every Thursday morning in the Trident base. Since then, we've begun to leaflet workers at the Keyport Torpedo Station, and the shipyard. Every week we pass out five hundred to a thousand leaflets. We've done that for almost five years in a row now, every week.

We try to develop a relationship of mutual respect and a dialogue
through the leaflets. We don't just try to propagandize. On various occa-
sions we'll pass out something different. We pass out valentines on Valen-
tine's Day; Thanksgiving Day we pass out loaves of bread. Sometimes we
pass out buttons that say, "I'd rather make toys". We try to keep varying
what we pass out. We pass out cartoons and all kinds of odd things.

We feel that every worker, whether he or she takes a leaflet or not, is an
important person and a person we have to respect, regardless of what
their attitudes are. We find that even with those who are most hostile to us,
there tends to be a mellowing process that goes on over the days and
months and years. Because it's been years now.

A lot of the naval personnel have changed. We've run through five or six
base commanders since we began. As you stay around that long, and you
express friendship toward other people, they begin to understand that it
isn't an attitude of being over or against them. So as time goes on they
have less of an attitude of being over or against us. And as we overcome
that attitude, which is what sustains the fence between Ground Zero and
the inside of the base, they begin to hear the questions that we're raising.

Unless we can overcome the attitude of alienation and of over or against,
the question can't be heard and can't be shared. That's the first thing that
has to be built upon. One of the most important parts of this work is building up that relationship.

We hold meetings in houses, house meetings like the farm workers do
where we try to talk to people who are most hostile to us. We'll go to a
church and ask people in the church if they would have a day of recollection
or reflection on Trident nuclear weapons, which often is refused.

But we often meet people who are supportive, one or two or three
people, and then we ask if they would hold a meeting in their home. Then
we talk to people whom they invite into their homes. It's real hard to get
people together, because talking about peace here is like talking about
Jewish people next to Auschwitz. It's the same reality. It's very, very
threatening in Kitsat County. People realize it's their bread and butter
that's at issue.

We tell our own stories. We don't begin by bringing up questions. We
begin by sharing our lives. Because there is a sense in which every worker
who goes into that base knows the questions. And it's not so much the
question – the people know the questions to some extent, but they don't
know the hope. They don't know the possibility of change. They don't know
the powers of miracles in their lives. They don't know that transformation
is possible.

Everybody's for peace, but none of us is willing to recognize the depth of sacrifice necessary to grasp peace. There is a security individually and personally that corresponds to the national security state. In order for us to be able to choose a nuclear-free world, we have to choose things like risking or giving up jobs, going to jail, suffering ridicule by our neighbors, losing political office. These are the kinds of sacrifices that should be understood as normal in a situation which is the most serious crisis in the history of humankind. We are on the verge of exterminating life. And unless we can give up all those forms of death that sustain it, which include things very close to us, to all of us. For example, one of the main sources of the nuclear arms race is the family, because of the attitudes of security that are bound up with the nuclear family.

People are for peace, except when it comes to giving up life insurance policies or bank accounts for their children's college educations. We always put it in terms of other people. We don't often put it in terms of ourselves. The most common way of putting it is in terms of my family or my children, the future of my children. If you're blinded by affluence, which we are in this country, and if you don't see any real hope in the power of nonviolence, the attitude becomes one of "I can't give up these things that my children need." That's understood in terms of affluence, and it wouldn't do any good anyhow because . . . these are forms of death. They're forms of spiritual death. And if we can't believe in the power of nonviolence, then we are accepting a process that's far worse than anything that the Third Reich was involved in. What they were able to do is miniscule next to what we are engaged in doing right now. These boxcars and these shipments that come by our house represent . . . the White Train that arrived March 22 had at least one hundred hydrogen bombs in it, perhaps two hundred. That goes far beyond the ten million the Third Reich destroyed.

If we continue to be passive cooperators in nuclear extermination than that's what would happen. Noncooperation with evil, as Gandhi taught, is as much a duty as cooperation with good. Which means that we must refuse to pay taxes that go to nuclear war; we must refuse to be silent when these kinds of shipments go by our homes. We must speak up in every way possible against that kind of buildup to a first-strike nuclear war. We must refuse to work in jobs that in any way sustain that kind of operation, no matter what that means to our own futures. We must be prepared to go to jail because of the terrible crime that's being committed in our name and with our cooperation. Those are all things that, unless we can do them and take responsibility for these weapons ourselves, will lead to an inconceivable slaughtering in a relatively short time.

Nuclear weapons are no accident. We need them. If you have 6 percent of the human species in control of approximately 40 percent of the earth's resources, you need nuclear weapons. It's no accident. It's a neccessary component of the situation of radical injustices. So a conversion deeper than the kind that we ordinarily understand politically is necessary to do away with nuclear weapons. It requires a transformation of the world, and especially of the attitudes in this country which sustain the arms race more deeply than attitudes anywhere else in the world.

The power of nonviolence is infinite because it is the power of God. The two aren't distinct. The way Gandhi described that power in its revelation is through experiments. He talked about experiments in truth. The power of nonviolence is revealed or comes home to us through personal and social experiments in its reality. Which I think Jesus was talking about when he said the Kingdom of God is at hand. That the power of nonviolence is no farther away than your or my hand. But we have to experiment in it, we have to try it out, we have to deepen it. So in here, we're constantly seeking new kinds of actions and new ways to explore that power that always requires our taking a further step. For example, what we're doing now is exploring the power of nonviolence along these tracks. That's the most recent development in the Trident campaign.

In 1981, as part of a workshop at Ground Zero, we had a pilgrimage around the base where we stopped at various points and meditated on what was represented here and how it related to us personally. When we go to these tracks at the end of the pilgrimage, I shared what I knew of the trains that came in here bearing missile materials to the Trident base, and I compared those trains to the trains that traveled anonymously through Europe during the 1940s, and which the people did not respond to, and as a result, millions died in the Holocaust. I mentioned where these trains came from: a number come from Salt Lake City, Utah, and bear missile motors from the Hercules Corporation there, and I named a number of the towns on the route coming here. And it turned out that everybody in our workshop lived along the tracks of the route. So we formed a community at the end of that workshop and called it the Agape Community – the Love of God, hopefully moving through our lives in such a way that there could be a response in the different towns and cities along these tracks.

So part of our experiment in the power of nonviolence has been through the Agape Community trying to link through hope and through nonviolent action the towns and cities that are linked through tracks bringing the equivalent of the ovens at Auschwitz to the Trident base. We feel that in that case, people were being brought to an extermination system; in this case, there's an extermination system being brought to the people. But in both cases the process is one that's dependent on the silence and complicity of all of us along the tracks. So we have been working to overcome that, and we've held vigils, simultaneous vigils and progressive vigils along the tracks, and we've begun to hold civil disobedience actions along the tracks.

When we started the Trident campaign in '75 we had no idea that there would be people in all these towns and cities along the tracks that would be involved in this process. But as you take a step, like moving into this house, we didn't know what it would signify. It's just that if you live next to these tracks, it's a reality you can't ignore and it opens up another reality. So if you make a commitment to nonviolence and you take a step into it, then that opens up something new. That's the experiment in truth that Gandhi was talking about. You have to keep taking the next step. Once you stop taking steps, the new doesn't open up. But if you keep taking the next step, then the new opens up. And in turn, that widens the campaign. Because you meet all kinds of incredible people. And they become involved in the process. So the tracks, which we would never know about, really, unless we lived here, connect us up to thousands of people in different communities. And that in turn opens up to them the reality that's passing through their communities which they never would have seen otherwise. We get our hopes from both of those sources. The Kingdom of God is really a process. It's not an idea, it's a process, and it's at hand. And through that process we meet people who continually give us hope from the changes going on in their lives as they become involved in it, and we become involved further through them.

We're beginning to reach a situation where I think the government regards the area between the plants that make these weapons, and the base, as enemy territory, because they have to pass through the people. And that's what we want to happen. That the land be reclaimed as a nuclear-free land, and the government then realizes that the people – they already realize it, but that they realize it more and more – the people are the enemy. Because people will not tolerate these things when we see what they really are, as we look at them as they roll through our communities.

Mary Kay Henry

Mary Kay Henry's roots are pretty deep in the west. Born and raised on a ranch, a homestead, in southwestern Wyoming, most of her adult life has been in western Idaho, where she is a Benedictine sister.

30

Last spring I had to face up to the fact I was carrying around about fifty pounds of baggage I didn't need. Five-oh. I said to myself, There must be a way to return to the cosmos what belongs in the cosmos and not collect it for myself. In a whole sense, the way I enter into this culture of consumerism is by hoarding, and my body was a sign of that. I had stored up this extra stuff, and there would never be enough rainy days.

I had gone to a workshop where two people who work out of Ground Zero in Seattle made a beautiful point in saying that the way we come toward nonviolence is by being direct and open and straightforward. What I realized in trying to let go of this excess weight was I needed to do that with others, to say that's what I'm doing. I needed to let myself give this back where it belongs. I don't own this.

I realized I needed to exercise my body, and when I first started doing that I went about it in a violent way. I will run this far this day. And it will be like this. Then through reflection and being with that, I came to understand that maybe my body had the message to give that back. I didn't have to take it away. That my body, too, was in harmony and I didn't need being violent to it. And so in the course of the year, I experienced an ability to eat sensibly, to eat healthy foods, and I came to a real delight in sharing meals with people. I've always liked to cook, and I appreciated preparing food.

It's probably no accident that we're the fast-food society. We seldom take time to cook. We don't take time for meals with each other. And so we have to defend ourselves from each other. If I cannot eat with you and converse with you, if I don't know your story, then I might treat you to a hamburger, but it'll be fifteen minutes and that's over. And you better get back to work, and I better get back to work because we have to make more money for the next hamburger. And if we cannot, on the international level, engage the Russian people in a banquet – whatever that would be – then we've got to bomb the hell out of them. Because they're our enemies. It's either/or.

If we don't have fellowship, then we have enmity. If I will not take the flavor of the Russian culture and tradition and reverence and digest and

welcome that, then I will hate them. I'll be afraid of them. I will come over
to my own society, build up this great banquet, and eat by myself. I'll build
up this great military defense, which is all about big bellies – body armament is also the armament in the arms race.

During the past year I've begun making connections between spiritual-
ity and the food we take in. In our Christian tradition particularly, we
think that God is present among us as food. Our liturgies are about God
present as food and sharing food – not just as Christians, but as human
beings connected with the things of the earth. Food is what we glean from
the earth. And so how we eat it is how we pray, how we relate, how we are
in the world. If I think the world belongs to me, then I can just consume it
and it's mine. Whereas if I belong to the cosmos, then I'm also food for
others. I'm available for others. I'm fruitful for others.

How I am in my own physical being is how I am in the community, with
my friends. How I am with them is very much how I am in my politics, how
I look for leadership. Do all the parts have something to contribute, or is it
only the head that's going to control?

I think the arms race has so much to do with our sexuality. I think, too,
in the arms race, we get unconnected from our bodies. Sexuality is about
vulnerability, about body-to-body revealing. It's about relationships, and to
me, the arms race is about nonrelationships. If I won't eat with you, and I
won't tell you my story, then it's prostitution to engage with you sexually.
If I've eaten with you and I've told you my story and we celebrate that,
then sexuality has meaning. Otherwise you make the other an object, and
there's no relationship, no sharing of person.

Are we going to allow ourselves, individually and as nations, to remain
isolated and in competition? We've become so accustomed to our lifestyle,
so many of us have become unthinking. We don't even realize that the way
we consume things has an impact on the fact that other people are starving.

I take for granted the things I have, and I know I can just get more. I
spend very little time wondering where my next meal is coming from. And
so I spend very little time wondering where my brothers and sisters in
Central America are eking out their next meal.

Might is right. We assume we have a right to control other people, a right
to have power over people. Where's our worth? How many people are working under you? God, nobody should be working under anybody. That's
another sexual image. We need to be working with people. How many
people do you work with? How many people do you play with? Not, how
many people are you over? If I have a right to be over you and control you,
then the United States has a right to control Guatemala, Nicaragua and
El Salvador. If I don't have a right to be over you, then we don't have a right

to go there.

At the same time I don't have a right to be over you. I need to be connected with you. I need to be caring about your story, your journey and your power. If I know that, then, as the United States, we have a lot. We need to be engaged in Central America, engaged there to enable. That might mean staying out of there and just standing by – we might need to be cheerleaders. Even to carry the ball a little bit. But only to enable. And that's the hardest, hardest thing. Enablement is about letting go. To enable you means you're going to be able to do something better than I can do it, or as well as. And then I won't be over you.

In our culture, our economic, our political . . . all our systems are built on competition. I'm beginning to question that. I'm not sure that the American way of life really needs to be built on that. Maybe we could have successful government, even representative government, without great competition. What if we called forth politicians who had enabled the community to grow? Instead of a person who was going to compete and control other people.

I think when we talk about peace, we're always talking about letting go. For me to be at peace with you means I need to let go of my assumptions at least to the degree that I welcome yours. If I have determined how the world's going to be, and you've determined that it's another way, there won't be peace until I can let go of mine and say, You're a gift. Then we'll probably discover our differences are more paradox than contradiction. We can both exist and make each other richer. But there's something in us that says either you're right or I'm right. Letting go is about saying, I know something and you know something, and together we know something that's different from what you and I know separately. And it's richer.

When I let go of all these things I think are so important, you might not respect that and you might attack me, and I might get hurt. And I probably will. So peacemaking is about dying. Probably where people engaged in peace movements become violent is because they don't understand that. They don't understand that letting go is about giving away your life, and that no one's going to say thank you for doing it. It's so hard, and yet so disarming.

I think many people come to the peace movement from the outside. We need a cause; we need to be dedicated to something; we've all this energy. To me, the groups that have been effective are those whose members have interiorized, become peaceful people inside. Out of that inner peacefulness, the direction goes. I also believe that if you have a core group who are really peaceful in their centers, then others coming at it more from the outside can be sustained by that group.

David Oien

Dave and Sharon Oien and their baby live in the house they built on the family farm near Conrad, in far-northern Montana. He was raised on the farm, and his parents still farm and live here, too. Dave has also built a production size solar greenhouse and is just about ready to come on line with full-scale methane conversion. His interest in renewable energy and "appropriate" technology was a few years ahead of his neighbors; he hopes his concern for demilitarizing Montana is too.

31

My interest in renewable energy and alternative technology and the antinuclear movement is really centered in a concern for the earth and a conversion I had a number of years back. What moved me is some understanding of the spirit of the earth, and being somewhat opposed to the spirit of high technology and the technologically-oriented society. Being raised here as a farmer, as a farm kid, I sort of had my feet in both worlds from the beginning. A real strong literal connection to the earth, and also an understanding of machinery, of technology, of technics.

Out here we farm with large-scale equipment, and we absolutely depend upon machinery. We depend upon – at least in the past – petroleum fuels to make farms work. Somewhere along the line, it was important for me to piece it together. The earth and the technologies. It was important to live a life that had as little adverse effect on the planet as possible. Because it seems to me that we owe the planet something; we owe the earth something as a sustainer of us. There is something very foreign about having missile silos located on farmland in Montana. They are out of place. They are instruments of death by design, and I think they are also symbols of death in all of our psyches, whether or not we admit that. They represent death, and are placed on land, in land, that at least to me is a place of life. Agriculture.

These weapons have a dulling effect on our humanity. Just the fact that they are there is an intrusion upon the humanity of Montanans, and whoever else has to live with them. They were placed here basically against our will. I think most of us out here are peaceful people, and would at least like to be understanding people. We're quite tolerant people, in spite of our provincialism. People are very proud to be here, proud to be Americans. Most of us here are homesteaders who came from somewhere else, and we're of different nationalities. We are not natives here. I think hidden in that is a bit of tolerance. Many people around here are of Russian descent. We're of Norwegian descent. Our neighbors are of German descent. I like to think all of us living here together allows us an ability to say, Wait a minute, aren't we all human beings on this planet? Can't we all somehow get along?

An interesting thing is that in all the communities around here there is a very small number of people who are the antinuclear movement. A handful of people: three or four, five in a community of three or four thousand, in spite of the fact that missiles surround these communities. Whereas if you go to Helena or Missoula, cities that are further removed, there is, per capita, much greater involvement. Why is that? I'm not sure, but I think part of it is that we are numbed by their very presence. We don't dare either admit or take seriously the destructive power they have, because if we did it would drive us berserk.

Probably the same thing happened in World War II to people who lived next to the death camps or along the route of the trains taking people to the death camps. I suspect people there could not admit it to themselves that it existed. What was taking place. But somehow they knew it. Looking at a similar situation here in Conrad, in Shelby, in Chester, if you talk to people on a one-to-one basis and in a private setting, people will admit they do not like the military presence here. They do not like the missiles that are here. But it's also impossible to get them to write a letter to the editor of the paper, come to a meeting, or give any other hard support to the antinuclear movement. And that's distressing to those of us who have chosen to take a public voice.

I think there is an effect, just of the missiles being here. When a convoy goes through town, eighteen vehicles long, taking up a mile of traffic, and right in the center is a nuclear warhead that – the Minuteman III has three separate warheads on it – could conceivably destroy millions of people easily right in the first blast, that reaps a terrible toll on all of us.

Recently there was a meeting with the Air Force about a B-52 practice run planned for an area out east of town. The place was packed, but only two or three of us questioned the need or the intelligence of running the bombers here and the adverse effects it could have to livestock, farmers, and the psychological well-being of residents. The representative of the Chamber of Commerce stood up and said, Well, we for one, in contrast to these guys over here, will be very glad to see this happen because we would have fifty more residents in town. Fifty more people would be buying carpets, fifty more buying food. Underneath it all, I think basic greed is operating. Or self-interest, personal interest. People don't really believe that these things are ever going to be fired. So we might as well take advantage of it, right? The government spends X billions of dollars; we might as well get some of it. It's good for the economy; war's good business. And even peace is good business the way we conduct it now.

In my cynical moments I say that the only way to get large numbers of people interested in shutting down one missile silo, or in general disarm-

ament, is to boil it down to economics. If we could show the residents of
Conrad that it was costing them X thousands of dollars a year, leaving this
community, producing nothing to the GNP or the welfare of the country,
I think all of a sudden you're going to be talking about having some
converts.

You can look back fifteen years to the Vietnam War. Many times I con-
sole myself by saying it was those people who were marching in the
streets, those of us who burned our draft cards, it was all those people that
shut down the war. I think that was a contributing factor, but I also think
we got to the point it was costing just too damn much, and the American
people said our taxes are going up. This is an expensive proposition; we're
not getting any gain out of it. Let's shut down this war. I think that's what
has to come as far as nuclear missiles go. People don't seem to have developed a sense of the terror they represent.

One of my greatest fears is that it will get ever and ever closer to me, to
this farm. We have no missile silos on our farm. We are on no roads by
which the missiles pass or the military convoys go. Occasionally now there
is a Huey flying over. I fear that ever more and more there is an increasing
military presence in this area. I can remember when there were no missile
silos. When I was in school, the building of the Minuteman was a big deal,
there was a huge influx of people, and we had to put up with it. Then there
was the ABM thing, and we had to put up with it. The thing just isn't going
away. There's always more, always more. Tomorrow, what else?

In the end, I'm a very conservative person in that I sort of like things – I
like this farm as it is, in its integrity. For instance, we won't sign an oil
lease because we don't want the encroachment. Because that means huge
equipment coming in, people making decisions that should not be made.
This is a very small farm in this area, 240 acres. Many people, especially
out east of town, the drylanders, are one thousand, two, three thousand
acres. In a way maybe what's at the bottom of my fear is that it is small,
that we can look out the window and see all our land. That's fine with me.
I don't want to buy more land. I don't want the neighbor to go broke and
me take over so I can make more money. I think a farm this size should be
able to support twelve to fourteen people. There's no reason it can't.

My hope goes back to the spirit of the earth in that somehow things survive. Somehow the planet has been here for so long and has survived an
awful lot of catastrophes. At bottom I may not even have all that much
hope for the human species, but I have a lot of hope for the planet because
the sun comes up every day, plants grow in the spring. A nuclear holocaust
would change those things dramatically. However, living on the farm it's
almost as if no matter how much damage you happen to do one season,

you plant the wrong crop or whatever happens, things come back. Things survive. And I think there's something operating here, if we look at it in the long run . . . I have a lot of friends in town who live from week to week or month to month depending on when the paycheck comes in. Their cycles, at least to me, seem rather short. Here we live season to season, year to year, and even sometimes in three- or four-year runs. Two years ago we were hailed out. So you have to sort of look beyond. Being a farmer allows me the liberty of looking further beyond.

Marvin Kammerer

*Elk Creek Valley lies about ten miles north of Rapid City, South Dakota, as the crow
flies. About two thousand acres of the valley, a smaller ranch in these arid parts, was
homesteaded by Marvin's grandfather, who came here almost directly from Germany.
Today, most of the valley is under the domain of the U.S. government, as the home
of Ellsworth Air Force Base. The Kammerer ranch abuts the base, and in fact, this
has been a point of contention in several legal disputes. The Kammerers have six
children of assorted ages; the youngest two still ride their horses to the one-room
schoolhouse their grandfather helped build.*

32

I was in court with the U.S. government in 1980 because I wouldn't sign an easement up here giving them further use of the land. We brought in a noise expert, who had worked for NASA, the Navy, the Army, to testify on our behalf. He said excessive noise level has an effect on everyone and everything; to what extent is yet to be proven. I do not know what that effect may be. I may not be getting as many pounds on my livestock that I sell. The conception rate may not be as good. I don't know these things. But the easement they took restricted my use and gave them use in perpetuity. They're the only ones that talk about easements in perpetuity. You just try to get one.

Here's where the B-52s take off from and fly around this country. I've seen two broken arrows. That is the mistake they didn't know was a mistake. These things take off and you know something's wrong. Their bellies are full. And all over the world those planes are doing it at the same time. It's scary.

There was one morning about three years ago that I knew in my guts there was something wrong . . . it took me a long time before I even talked about that with anyone, let alone my family. It was about nine in the morning, and man, the buggers came over, the black smoke just pouring out like a cannon. They were loaded. One after the other. I knew something had gone wrong. Then it dawned on me, This is for real. Here's two of my kids riding to school down here. And I'm wondering, what is it, fifteen minutes – the warning – or a half hour? Is that the last that I see of those kids? My oldest daughter in the valley with one child at that time. My brothers and sisters in the area, my kids at the high school in Spearfish. And my wife at work. My mother and father in Montana. Minutemen all around there. That's Ground Zero area. My sister in Montana. My brother. All of those. All Ground Zeroes. Friends, children. Russian children.

I found out about two weeks later that it was nothing but a screw-up on the part of the electronics that tells us whether or not missiles are coming.

I've lived a pretty good life as far as enjoying the simple things. I'm not afraid for my own life. A horse could kick me in the head tomorrow and that's all right. But when we lower this time down, say with the MX or the Poseidon, the chance of error multiplies. Your time to correct it is not there any more. You don't have that leeway. Or what if one leader or the other would happen to have a bad day? Or go off the deep end? Or gets drunk?

This is where they store the warheads that are not already in the silos on missiles. They replace these things periodically and ship them around. Weinberger's trying to say our system's all out of date. Well, in fact these systems were all modified in the late seventies, and they're lying to us, lying to the American people. And it's time that the American people start thinking that elected officials are not necessarily responsible people. In fact, sometimes they have their own axle to grease – like Bechtel; look who most of Reagan's top defense advisors are.

They build them. Bechtel is mixed up in the missile development system all around the world, and that's where Weinberger and Shultz and Habib and all those guys come from. Based in California, old Steve Bechtel and these guys are all old buddies. They charge whatever we're willing to pay, and even more.

The military has changed in my lifetime. During World War II there were a few guys out here that were kind of wild, but a lot of them were interested in you, too, and they'd come for dinner. We had a different relationship than we do now.

At the end of World War II when they were changing the name from War Department to Department of Defense, there was quite a debate. Vandenburg was a senator then (later he got a base named after himself), and one of his statements was – to keep all this apparatus going – We're going to have to scare the hell out of the American people in order to get them to buy it, to accept it. That's when the Cold War set in. For thirty-five, forty years we've lived in this, and it's got progressively worse. It hasn't gotten us any more security by being the most heavily armed nation in the world.

People like me are the next Indians. We occupy this land that was occupied by Indians before us. But we are the next Indians unless we change things around, and Indian people know that. They realize the government sets policies that allow exploitation of the land. To people who have power, who have money, it's a game. So we who are on the land now, if we don't change the policies, and if our government does not correctly start owning up to its responsibilities of protecting its people, then the corporate interests are going to own agriculture.

I'm already the victim of the arms race. We have to borrow money to run our ranch, in order to operate and to live until the next pay, which is about once a year. And who's our biggest competitor who drives up interest in the money market? Uncle Sam. He's the biggest borrower of all. Continuing the arms race is going to do nothing but escalate the government's need to compete with me in the money market. I can't survive against that.

If I'm lucky enough, I'll end up with a piece of paper that says I own this ground I occupy. The ranch. But in essence, the ground owns me. I can't sell it because that would be like selling my mother. The fact that it's treated me well. We don't live in a fancy home or anything, but we have a good life with family, friends. It's always home to no matter who comes by – a sharing of what we live in. That should be an attitude that we look on the land as, not something to exploit and take from all the time, not giving anything back. When I leave this land I hope it is in as good or better shape than when I took it over from my father. That means it's going to survive.

We've got to own up to the responsibility of stewardship. People say, Well, I own this land. I have a right to do this and this and this. That is a misconception. We do not have a right to exploit the land. We do not have the right to abuse the land, thus weakening the chance of future generations to survive. With every right comes a responsibility.

There are many people out here in this country who are very poor, but they can always look down their noses at the Indian. At least they are better than that. The same was true in the South when the redneck poor white, no matter how tough his state of life was, at least he could always figure, I'm better than that black bastard.

That whole concept keeps us from coming together and exchanging ideas as to where the real problem lies. While we wrangle around with one another, multinational corporations like Bechtel, Kerr-McGee, United Fruit, Citibank – these guys have their own games going. It's very clear to me what's going on in Central America. There's no doubt in my mind whose side I'd be on if I were one of those people down there. Because I *understand* why we had a revolution. We were tired of being exploited, wanted to run our own affairs. How can we sit here and bless Polish Solidarity and at the same time condemn people who are trying to get the same in central America? If we keep operating the way we are down there, we'll have more Cubas. It's guaranteed.

The United States and other governments always are hollering for peace. We like peace, but on our terms only. It's like the mentality of the man who's training young horses. Rather than trying to understand that horse as a creature with a mind and instincts, they are impatient like overgrown boys who have a problem of a bully instinct in them. So they want to beat them around to make them do what they want.

It's not easy to admit you've made a mistake; it's a weakness in this country. We've never apologized to the Japanese people for their internment during World War II. My father always said—he had trouble doing it himself—a man who can own up to his own mistakes, he's a man. But it's not easy to do. We all have a certain machismo, women included. And we haven't grown up enough to deal with that, to say, I'm sorry, I goofed. If we're able to live with our neighbors across the fence . . . if I make a mistake, I try to atone for it. Say, I'm sorry I did that, I won't let it happen again. And we patch up our differences because we're both occupying the same area. We've got to get along.

I enjoy getting up in the morning. That's the best time of the day for me. When the birds are talking to me and talking to themselves. The air is the freshest. If I want to sit down and talk or sit down at noon and not do a damn thing, I can do it. I still have freedom to choose to do that, and I enjoy it. People give me energy. These kids. I don't go full bore all the time. Can't do that. You've got to pace yourself as to where you want to go, and how you're going to get there. And you can't change the world overnight or next week. It isn't going to happen. An old Chinese proverb says it takes a hundred years to change a man. So let's not get too impatient.

I hope most of the world has a little patience with the United States. She's a very young country, and she certainly has problems with machoism and all this crap. But people eventually will boot that mentality out, not admitting they've made a mistake. I hope the world has a little patience with us.

Brian Palecek

Artist, poet, classical musician, author, community organizer and state coordinator for the nuclear freeze referendum, Brian Palecek of Bismarck, North Dakota, is also the active and concerned parent of three young children.

33

When I started, I was very hesitant about using the word *peace*. In fact, a really important part of my own meditation process was involved with the discipline of folding paper cranes. The tradition of the Japanese — you fold a thousand paper cranes and you get a wish.

I decided that I would fold a thousand paper cranes for the same reason Sadako did and a lot of other people did, for peace. I didn't even want to say the word *peace* because it didn't mean that much. It seemed so wishy-washy. What I realized I was wishing for was some kind of a rising up of the people, standing up and confronting the issue of nuclear threat and arms race, standing up in a bold and courageous way to wrestle with the issue. That's what I was wishing for.

I didn't know what the outcome would be; I didn't know what vision of peace would occur. I try to be very, very practical at the same time that I try to draw on a kind of mystical vision. My actions have to be practical because I work in the community, North Dakota, as a political person. I work directly with people and try to articulate and interpret peace in a very practical way.

My son, Justin, my daughter and I went to New York City and were in the rally there on June 12. So I've experienced a million people standing up, and in that my wish was coming true. The wish for standing up and confronting the issue. By now I've folded 523 cranes, so I haven't reached my thousand, but in the process, I'm now clearer that I can start articulating a vision of what peace might mean in a situation.

I think the chief deterrent of nuclear war, since the beginning, has been the moral deterrent. And that is never given any attention. That's a nice way to increase your military budget because you can say, well, the credit for the peace is military, and so if you don't have it, in fact the world may come to an end if you don't make this new weapon, this MX or this Star Wars. So the arms deterrent has been the one that gets all the credit, and most people actually believe it. But I believe that since the beginning of this age, after the bombing of Hiroshima and Nagasaki, the most important deterrent has been moral.

Very simply it is the idea that's expressed over and over by poets and artists and writers and political leaders, too, that nuclear war is a b*aaaa*d thing. It is something that should never happen again, and if anyone does it he would go down in history as a b*aaaa*d, bad person. So for forty years, we've been living in this situation in which the human race actually has been expressing an opposition to the further use of nuclear weapons pretty loud and clear, even though we're not clear that we actually do it. It never gets much attention. But we do have a moral teaching and tradition that says don't you ever do this again. No one since 1945 has used it, even though the United States very seriously has considered using nuclear weapons ten times but was deterred. Over and over, the use of nuclear weapons was deterred because the leaders knew that if they were used there would be a great outcry.

This spring, Churchwomen United decided to sponsor a bus tour of North Dakota, to travel in their own state, explore their own community more deeply, to see what happens here. Sister Marjorie Truite and I were the tour guides.

As we traveled between towns, we stopped in various towns and visited social service institutions that dealt with child abuse, wife abuse, rape, senior citizens and the handicapped. We stopped at the air force base in Minot, and talked with one of the leaders. We stopped at a missile site, got out and inspected that, and took pictures of it. The whole thing was a study tour, but it evolved into a pilgrimage, into a deeper sense of one's own community. Since we were traveling through a lot of land, we had many chances to actually explore new ways of seeing our own land.

One important image that a person used was the paradox about the same field having the potential to feed the hungry of the world, and the fact that the field also contained the most destructive force human beings have ever created. A field with the beautiful, tilled soil, sprouts coming up, and right in that field is a missile silo. That paradox is very important. Just the word silo, for instance. We use the word silo to describe the missile silo. But what is a silo? It's something you put grain in. You put grain in silos to store it for people to use.

Another very important part of what happened was the beginning of a discussion of the relationship between sexuality and the arms situation. Sister Marjorie at the very beginning of our trip started talking in terms of male dominance, patriarchy, rape and child abuse and wife abuse.

I've come to think one of the great issues in the arms race is the rediscovery of male sexuality separate from violence and warfare. It's one of the great struggles of humanity at this time. The reassessment of what male sexuality is about, separate from the war tradition and the violence tradition. The questions of impotence and sexuality, power and self-esteem. As a community organizer, I have to take these questions into consideration. When I'm talking with men, the soldiers, I know I have to be sympathetic with all the levels of their psyches, as much as I possibly can.

The real challenge is anything now dealing with peace has to be as potent and as vital, as ceremonially exciting as the war tradition has been. Marching bands, dance, ceremony, symbol, uniform or whatever. All the paraphernalia that have been associated with the grand tradition of militarism – the peace movement has to be every bit as potent. People ask me, Do you think movies like *Star Wars* make us more warlike? I have to answer, My children have seen those movies and enjoyed them, particularly my boys. They come home playing laser beam, shooting and zapping people. But I also know that my sons, all my children, experience work for peace which has equal time or more to the fun they have with weaponry and war. It has to be at least equal. For every hour that you spend on a video game that has guns shooting, consider an hour on things dealing with cooperation, harmony, joy, the work of justice and the like. If you don't, if your child doesn't have that equal time, then you can say it is hurting him. I have no doubt about that. But if they do both, then you can say that they're wrestling with it and getting something done.

During the freeze campaign I saw this beautiful experience of children handing out brochures and flyers and things like that. And I knew that they were having a powerful experience working on disarmament and peace. Things that repudiated weapons. That same child might go out to see *Star Wars* and be excited by it – and I do, too. I think it's powerful. But at least he had some concrete and real sense. He may have made cranes; he's heard the story of Sadako; he knows that weapons kill people, kill children with leukemia, all sorts of things, even many years afterwards.

It's paradoxical to watch this, in my boys in this case, this tension between being very much peace-oriented people, knowing that work of peace is possible, disarmament is good, that nuclear weapons are bad. At the same time, being a person who's right now in his own life debating whether he should go hunting this fall. His grandfather likes to hunt, is a good hunter, and I respect him as a hunter. He's a wonderful teacher for my son. And yet my son now is wondering, Maybe I don't really want to kill the ducks. He's making his own kind of moral judgement. He's nine. He has to make that judgement, and I respect that. I love to watch the process, be part of it and not try to manipulate him either way.

One of the things I'm working on right now is a children's book, actually a coloring book, called *A Letter to the Emperor*. What it does is retell the freeze campaign, the freeze referenda in which people sent a message to the president, in the fairy tale mode. The story basically is about these two empires, their emperors, and wanting more weapons all the time. The people in the story – it's sort of like North Dakota with farms and fields – get together and say something's got to change. This can't go on forever. What shall we do? They debate and they argue. They decide they could send a letter to the emperor asking him to talk with the other emperor about a mutual, verifiable freeze.

The tension of the story is, Should we send this letter? Because that's what this community is debating and discussing. We weren't ending the arms race; all we were debating for a two-month period was, Should we send this letter? To the emperor. That's all. And the reason I was so conscious of this is because people would ask me, What are we voting on exactly? I mean, is this to close down the army or something? No, I had to be very precise. What we're doing, what we're trying to do, is decide whether you want to send this letter or not. And you either have to vote yes or no. Or abstain.

Ruth Carey

Ruth Carey, public health nurse and teacher of nursing in Ann Arbor, Michigan, speaks out forthrightly about the suffering she and her students encounter daily. After a quarter-century in her work the connection between poverty and the arms race is inescapably clear.

34

The work that I do is with people who suffer. That's what the public health nurses do. They work with families who are economically, culturally deprived. Poor people, for the large part. I've worked with those people since 1960. And what I see is that the quality of life for the poor is so affected by the priorities that this country sets up. And so if our priority is on building hardware for war, I see people who now can't get adequate food for their babies, who don't have access to medical care because the eligibility for department of social services is lower than it used to be, or elderly people who don't have adequate assistance because the Food Stamp program is cut back. That's why it's a part of a much larger issue for me. I think it's related to racism, sexism and economic deprivation.

The places where I work, and work with students, are two. Washtenaw County and the county southwest of us, Lenawee. In Lenawee County there's a town of about twenty thousand people, and the rest is rural; Washtenaw County has Ann Arbor and Ypsilanti and then some small villages. Poverty is more pronounced in Lenawee County; there are many, many rural poor there. There's a high Mexican-American population, about 15 percent, and those people by and large are really poor. But in Ann Arbor we see it just as well. There are people who have difficulty meeting the food needs of their families, who have difficulty having adequate heat and paying their rent. And I can't–I can't believe that the needs of those people cannot be easily cared for if our monies were budgeted with a priority of quality of life. How can we say we value all the people in this country and cut away what it is that makes life livable for the poor?

You go into these homes where stresses are incredibly high. The husband has no job, or has a job he hates, a job that doesn't pay enough money to provide what he needs for his family. So he's got his own stresses. And you've got a wife who has no freedom at all. I mean, she is owned practically. This is so common. She has no life of her own in terms of the clarity of her own journey or any of that. And trapped economically as well, because there's not enough money for anything. And then he has the power to physically abuse her, and he does. It's an explosive situation.

I understand a lot of the societal reasons for why he behaves that way. But to me, those are evidences of a violent society. And so the violence, the domestic violence that happens regularly in our culture, is part of what I see the national violence being, making war, and it seems to me like it's a piece of the same fabric. It's a way we view life in this country. Whether it's a formal military action called war, or whether it's a person who has the power over someone else, physically beating them or psychologically oppressing them. Whether it's an employer doing that to an employee, or whether it's a husband doing that to a wife and children. It's domination, power over.

My specific interest in the nuclear power and war issue both – and my whole concern about war – is relatively new. I did not grow up in a pacifist family. My father was not in the war, but it was because of a physical deferment. My uncles were all in the Army or the Navy, and that was a really acceptable kind of thing. Well, that consciousness began to change during the Vietnam War, questioning of what is this country about over there in Southeast Asia. What were we doing? My myth about who this country is began to alter. I began to realize that what I'd always thought – that America did things that are good for other people – was no longer. It wasn't true, and I began to disbelieve that. And so I began to think differently about when this country makes war, why does it make war? It was a kind of slowly evolving thing.

I began to look at the whole issue of how I felt about war and what I believed about war. I have always had the position that there were just wars; that was how I came up. And in the last two or three years that has come under clear question inside of me. I'm becoming less and less able to believe in a just war theory, believing that violence . . . and I'm talking not about oppressed people now who do whatever they have to do to survive, but imperialist nation-states who make war on other nation-states. I'm having a really hard time believing that that's ever justified. There comes a point at which there is no coming back, having made war. To me, that is what the nuclear holocaust is about. There would never be the option of doing what we did in Vietnam, because there would be none of us left.

I can't conceive of any way in which I as a nurse would be able to assist people in any effective way, because it would be such a horrid disaster. There would be nothing that could be done. There would be no facilities in which to treat people. And there would be no health care practitioners available to do the treating if the facilities were there. And because of the destruction to the electrical and water systems, even if you had the facilities and the people, the infection rates would be incredible.

The Michigan Nurses Association was approached by PSR to cosponsor one of their workshops, and so we asked to participate in the program. I will be speaking on one of those agendas in Lansing in the spring, and what I'm going to talk about is not the medical aspects of nuclear war or all the other stuff that all those physicians already know. I'm going to talk about the effect of the nuclear arms buildup on the quality of life for people in our country. And what happens to these families that my students are visiting and doing nursing care with; what happens when they can't get food coupons for their babies. I'm going to talk about the rising infant death rate in inner city Detroit, and how it's inescapably the consequence of decisions made at the national level to build up military arms and to cut human service . . . to those children the holocaust has occurred.

Hannah Rabin

Along with two friends, Hannah and her sister, Nessa, began the Children's Campaign for Nuclear Disarmament in the kitchen of their Vermont farmhouse. They were fifteen and thirteen at the time. While living in France, with the L'Arche Community several years before, their father learned the trade of baking bread in an ancient stone oven. Behind the house, in a separate building, he has carefully crafted a similar oven. This is the family business.

35

We started two years ago. We were sitting around in somebody's kitchen and talking about our fears. We were really afraid. We thought we might not grow up, thought the world would probably be destroyed before we had a chance to live our lives. So we decided to do something. We thought that instead of just sitting around and talking among ourselves, we should find out what other kids were thinking and try to do something to influence the government to change the situation.

I think it has a lot to do with the way we were brought up. In this family and in two other families of kids that are involved, our parents have been active ever since we could remember. Against the Vietnam War, working for civil rights. We talked about politics all the time around the dinner table. I remember my father going to a demonstration in Washington, DC, and coming back, and he and my mother were talking about the Vietnam War. He said he was just in Washington, and I wanted . . . I said the next time he went to Washington, I wanted him to bite President Nixon.

I remember coming home after organizing three actions: Children's Walk for Life, June 12, and the letter writing campaign to President Reagan, which resulted in our going to Washington and reading the letters. I came home and broke down. I just couldn't do it any more. I was too exhausted. I think you have to keep a balance in your life. You can't just be a political activist. You've got to do some peace work every day, but you also have to do other things. You have to spend time with family and friends, and you have to read a little bit and work in the garden. And make time for things.

I wanted to drop out of high school just to do peace work because I felt the situation was so urgent. What can we do? We have to drop our lives and go running, like Helen Caldicott says. You've got to drop everything, run to the peace movement, because what's the point of anything else in life if the world blows up? And I agree with that. But I also think just the reverse. What's the point of having a peace movement, what's the point in saving the world if everybody's going to go batty trying to just do peace work? You've got to make peace work fun, and you've got to make a balance in your life. You can't always think of peace work as this terrible thing, a burden that you have to carry.

I remember being in New York in a public school, PS 84, with a group of second- and third-graders. We sat around and talked. We started off by talking about Hiroshima and Nagasaki. And why – what the government said, what the government's reason was for bombing. And is that really right to use people that way; getting into the moral questions. When the discussion got going, they were just furious. Little kids standing up and saying, How can these old men do this? They're going to ruin my life. One said, "I want to be a doctor when I grow up. How am I going to be a doctor if they're going to blow up my world?" They were really furious. I've been in classes where kids cry because they're so afraid. I think they have these fears all the time, but they haven't wanted to think about it. They haven't wanted to talk about it.

When we're visiting in classes kids suddenly realize they aren't alone, that other people are really doing something, that there's something hopeful to do. When we go into a class, we always do some kind of project. I remember telling them to come up and write "June 12, Be There" on the board. It was great, because they all said, "Oh yeah, we're going to go." They had something to think about. They would be able to do something. They were going to bring their friends and tell their parents to go. They really felt like they were going to make a difference. And they did make a difference, a small difference. There aren't any fewer bombs, but it did make a difference because it changed the minds of many people in this country. Even the government can't say anymore, "We're going to fight and win a nuclear war."

We wanted kids to write letters to President Reagan opposing the arms race, to send the letters to our office, and we'll take them and read them aloud in front of the White House and try to deliver them personally to the president. At first the letters just trickled in. We thought, Oh God, this is going to be a drag. We'll take twenty letters to the White House, read them aloud in ten minutes and the president isn't going to want to meet with us for just twenty letters. But then they started to pour in; we collected almost three thousand. We went to Washington, and we tried to make an appointment to meet with the president. We wrote him saying we would like to meet with him to deliver these letters. And we got a letter from his secretary saying, sorry, President Reagan will be busy at that time. He's too busy to meet with you. We weren't surprised at that, but we were still angry.

We were furious. We had come with almost three thousand letters which were the voices of many people in the United States. It was a runaround. I think the main thing we felt after that was the White House is really afraid. Which is a strange thing for adults to be afraid of kids. We were making such a simple plea. We were just asking for the right to grow up in a safe world. Such a simple thing, such a basic thing. And this administration is doing everything in its power to build up more nuclear weapons, which is making this world more unsafe than it's ever been.

I see the children's campaign as having a twofold purpose. One is to help kids deal with their fear, because I think fear in itself is very dangerous. It's a more difficult thing than I think adults can easily understand. Kids are scared right now that they won't grow up. And that's such a profound thing, such a deep thing, dangerous. For kids it's really feeling powerless, because they know the grown-ups are supposed to take care of the world a little better, and their parents are supposed to protect them. They feel cheated when their parents can't do anything, when they realize how powerless their parents alone are.

I think the campaign empowers kids. It gives them hope that they can do something. I was scared. I was a lot more scared and completely unable to deal with my fear before I started. When I started to do this work, I got caught up in it, and I got hope. I realized that there was something we could do. And that's really important. Also, I think kids have a tremendous amount of power to influence grown-ups and the people who are making decisions. Influence voters, influence grown-ups who can also join the peace movement, influence the government directly.

I think that kids will naturally plan actions they like. We've done things like we marched in the Fourth of July parade with big paper doves that we made a few days before, huge paper doves. They were sort of floppy; they were really beautiful. We cut poplar sticks with the leaves still on, and strung birds from them, and we marched with our banner and the birds. Lots of us. It was beautiful, and it was fun. There's a lot of ideas that kids have.

DATE DUE

HIGHSMITH # 45220